D1074374

HANS KUNDNANI

The Paradox of German Power

Oxford University Press is a department of the
University of Oxford. It furthers the University's objective
of excellence in research, scholarship, and education
by publishing worldwide.

Oxford New York
Auckland Cape Town Dar es Salaam Hong Kong Karachi
Kuala Lumpur Madrid Melbourne Mexico City Nairobi
New Delhi Shanghai Taipei Toronto

With offices in
Argentina Austria Brazil Chile Czech Republic France Greece
Guatemala Hungary Italy Japan Poland Portugal Singapore
South Korea Switzerland Thailand Turkey Ukraine Vietnam

Published in the United States of America by
Oxford University Press
198 Madison Avenue, New York, NY 10016

Published in the United Kingdom in 2015 by C. Hurst & Co. (Publishers) Ltd.

www.oup.com

Library of Congress Cataloging-in-Publication Data is available for this title
Hans Kundnani
The Paradox of German Power

ISBN 978-0-19-024550-4

Printed in the United States of America on acid-free paper

CONTENTS

ACKNOWLEDGEMENTS

I wrote this short book while working at the European Council on Foreign Relations (ECFR), to which I am indebted for providing me with a uniquely stimulating environment and for introducing me to thinkers and policymakers in Germany and the rest of Europe. Above all I would like to thank Mark Leonard, in particular, for prompting me to think about the concept of "geo-economics". I have also benefited hugely from discussions about Germany with other colleagues. In particular, I would like to thank Olaf Boehnke, Piotr Buras, Sebastian Dullien, Josef Janning and José Ignacio Torreblanca. I am also grateful to Alba Lamberti and Vessela Tcherneva for their support while I was working on the book.

Parts of the argument in this book were developed in essays that have been published in various journals in the last few years. I would like to thank Sylke Tempel and Rachel Herp Tausendfreund at *Internationale Politik*, Alexander Lennon at the *Washington Quarterly*, Lucio Caracciolo at *Limes*, Eric Langenbacher at *German Politics and Society* and Jörg Später at the *Journal of Modern European History*. Lucio and Rachel (now a colleague at ECFR) also made extremely useful comments on drafts of the book.

A number of other colleagues and friends also read earlier drafts and made extremely helpful comments. In particular, I would like to thank Sir Michael Arthur, Jakub Eberle, Geoff Eley, Dominik Geppert, Lord Stephen Green, Megan Greene, Almut Möller, Sebastian Płóciennik and Gary Savage. My own thinking has also benefited hugely from conversations with Geoff Eley, Hanns W. Maull, Thomas Kleine-Brockhoff, Daniela Schwarzer and Steve Szabo, Simon Tilford and Philip Whyte, among others.

ACKNOWLEDGEMENTS

I was prompted to write this book by Michael Dwyer and Brendan Simms, who have been extremely supportive from the beginning. I would also like to thank my editor, Georgie Williams, for her meticulous work on the text.

Finally, I would like to thank Angela Stanzel for her help with umlauts.

INTRODUCTION

THE RETURN OF HISTORY?

During the past two decades, German historians have described the postwar Federal Republic above all as an *Erfolgsgeschichte*, or "success story". They have told of how it emerged from the catastrophe of 1945 to become a successful democracy, how it atoned for the Nazi past and developed a liberal political culture, and how it became part of an integrated and interdependent Europe. The story culminated in, and was confirmed by, reunification in 1990—which followed the first peaceful and successful revolution in German history. The reunified Germany was, as Heinrich August Winkler put it, "a post-classical democratic nation among others, firmly integrated into NATO and the European Community".[1] Thus Germany had finally abandoned its *Sonderweg*, or "special path", and completed what Winkler called its "long road west": Germany's equivalent of Francis Fukuyama's idea of the "end of history".

Germany had had a complicated and ambivalent relationship with the West. Many of the ideas that were central to what Winkler has called the normative project of the West came from German Enlightenment thinkers such as Kant. And yet German intellectual history also included a darker current of nationalism that first emerged in the nineteenth century, became increasingly anti-Western, and culminated in Nazism and the Holocaust—what Winkler calls "the climax of the German rejection of the Western world".[2] It was only after the catastrophe of 1945, that Germany—or at least the western half of it—was fully integrated into the West and attained what Winkler calls "Western normality". Thus Germany was a paradox: it played a central role in developing the normative project of the West but also produced the most radical European challenge to it.[3]

What made reunification a completion of this "long road west" is that it was a Western solution to the German question. At the time of reunification, some had feared the so-called Berlin Republic would become less Western than the Bonn Republic. But, at least during the first decade after reunification, those fears did not become reality as Germany confirmed its commitment to the West. In particular, there seemed to be a symbiotic relationship between Germany and Europe: German reunification was only possible in the context of European integration and seemed to prove that "German problems can only be solved under a European roof," as Konrad Adenauer had famously put it. Conversely, reunification was also a catalyst for further European integration and in particular the creation of the euro. In 2000, Winkler could write that fears about Germany had lessened in the decade since reunification.[4]

However, since the euro crisis began in 2010, there has been a need for an epilogue to the triumphalist narrative of German post-war history. The crisis thrust Germany into an extraordinary—and, in the history of the EU, unprecedented—position. The whole of the eurozone looked to Germany—the largest creditor in a crisis of a common currency consisting of sovereign states—for leadership. But, fearing the emergence of a "transfer union"—that is, one in which fiscally responsible member states subsidise fiscally irresponsible member states—it has resisted a mutualisation of debt in Europe, and has imposed austerity on others in the eurozone in an attempt to make Europe "competitive". The approach has in some ways deepened rather than narrowed the divide between surplus and debtor countries: while unemployment in Germany has reached the lowest level since reunification, it has risen to extraordinary levels in the countries of the so-called periphery. The cost of adjustment in the single currency, Andrew Moravcsik writes, has been borne disproportionately by "the poor and the powerless".[5]

Against the background of this clash between creditor and debtor countries in the eurozone, collective memories from Europe's pre-1945 past have both informed the discourse and been instrumentalised by it. The most dramatic—but by no means only—example is the mutual animosity between Germany and Greece.[6] Memories in Greece of the wartime occupation, during which, according to the historian Richard Clogg, it had experienced "one of the worst famines in the modern history of

Europe", remain strong.[7] Since the crisis began, Greek newspapers have compared Chancellor Angela Merkel to Adolf Hitler. When Merkel visited Greece in October 2012, some protesters burned flags bearing the Nazi swastika, dressed up in Nazi uniforms and held banners with slogans such as "Hitler, Merkel—same shit", and 7,000 Greek police were needed to protect her.[8] Some Greeks are once again demanding war reparations—which, according to a government report published in 2012, amounted to up to €162 billion.

The question raised by the surge of such collective memories is whether history has returned to Europe. In other words, have some features of pre-1945 international relations in Europe returned? Or has the euro crisis perhaps revealed that international relations in Europe have not changed as much as had been previously assumed? Part of the reason it is difficult even to begin answering such questions is that it is difficult even to articulate current developments in Europe. While the mixture of visionary and bureaucratic language connected with the EU no longer seems to capture reality, the language of pre-1945 international relations appears to be entirely inappropriate. Nevertheless, there remains a sense that Europe's past has in some way re-emerged. As former Luxembourg Prime Minister Jean-Claude Juncker, now president of the European Commission, put it in 2013: "The demons haven't been banished."[9]

At the centre of the history that seems in some ways to have returned to Europe is the "German question". Almost seventy years after the end of World War II, German power—the subject of this book—is once again a subject of intense debate. In 1953 Thomas Mann famously called for a "European Germany" rather than a "German Europe", but since the crisis began, it has become commonplace to speak of a German Europe emerging from it. There has been much debate about actual or potential German "hegemony" and some have even perceived the emergence of a kind of German "empire" within Europe. While the protesters on the streets of Athens compared Merkel to Hitler, others saw in her tough response to the euro crisis a reversion of Bismarckian *realpolitik*. But while such terminology and such comparisons imply a parallel with the problem of German power before 1945, they obscure the differences between history and the current situation. The implication is simply that, as French President Nicolas Sarkozy is reported to have told a friend in 2010, the Germans "haven't changed".[10]

Germans, meanwhile, are offended and baffled by these perceptions of a return of history. Most see the country's pre-1945 history as simply irrelevant to the current crisis in Europe and some even see attempts to draw parallels between the two simply as a pretext for extortion. German politicians, diplomats and analysts point out that Germany has learned the lessons of its history—a part of the success story of the Federal Republic. They argue not only that the Germans have changed, but also that Europe has changed. In the context of the EU, foreign policy had to some extent become domestic policy. In other words, they maintain that there can be no problem of German power at all and concepts such as "hegemony" are simply anachronistic. Thus the debate about German power has so far been a polarised one. In the absence of agreement about whether German history is relevant at all, there has been little discussion of *how* exactly it might be relevant.

Alongside this debate about German power in Europe in the last few years, there has also been a debate about Germany's commitment to the West. In particular since Germany's abstention in the United Nations Security Council on military intervention in Libya in March 2011, when it aligned itself with the four BRIC countries (Brazil, Russia, India and China), some have wondered whether Germany is increasingly tempted to abandon the West and "go it alone". It was accused of failing to take responsibility for solving global problems and upholding Western norms, and of being a consumer rather than a producer of security. It seemed to many to seek above all to sell cars and machinery—in particular to China, with whom it appeared to have developed a new "special relationship". Thus whereas Germany was accused of throwing its weight around in Europe, it was accused of failing to pull its weight beyond Europe.

The criticism of German policy beyond Europe in the last few years, like the debate about German power within Europe, raises the question of the contemporary relevance of Germany's pre-1945 history. In some ways, German foreign policy outside of Europe seems to be the opposite of that of Germany before 1945. In particular, it has made a decisive break with militarism and rejects the use of military force as a foreign-policy tool. If Germany stands for anything apart from exports, it is "peace". Germany perceives itself as a "post-heroic" society. Some see in Germany's rejection of the use of military force a rejection of power projection altogether. In short, they argue that Germany has learned the lessons of its past. "Re-education worked!" a senior German politician told me in 2010.[11]

However, others have seen parallels with German foreign policy during the *Kaiserreich*. Some have suggested that Germany has returned to its *Mittellage*, or central location, between West and East, though in a globalised world the East now includes not only Russia but also Asia and, above all, China. Others have accused Germany of pursuing a *Schaukelpolitik*—a Bismarckian policy of shifting alliances. Others still have seen in its pursuit of markets beyond Europe for its exports a neo-mercantilist foreign policy. Each of these terms suggests in a different way that, in foreign policy at least, Germany is regressing and unlearning the lessons it has learned since 1945. So is Germany now in some way reversing its "long road west"?

In order to begin to answer these difficult questions, it is first necessary to understand what the "German question" originally was—and how it was answered after two world wars. In Chapter 1, therefore, I examine German foreign policy from 1871 to 1945. After unification in 1871, Germany's size and location—the so-called *Mittellage*—put it in a position of "semi-hegemony" in Europe that created instability in the international system. In other words, the "German question" was a structural one. But German foreign policy during this period was also informed by nationalism and in particular the idea of a "German mission"—what might be called ideology. This chapter is not intended to make an original argument about German history, but rather to outline developments and to summarise debates about the "German question".

In Chapter 2, I examine the foreign policy of the Federal Republic from its creation in 1949 to 1990. Though 1945 was not the "zero hour" that some imagined it was, it was nevertheless a break—in particular in German foreign policy. Though the Federal Republic is often thought of a "normative" or "civilian" power, such descriptions obscure the fault lines within West German foreign-policy debates. In particular, I identify two distinct currents in West German foreign policy during the period: an idealist one that began with Konrad Adenauer and the idea of the *Westbindung*, and a realist one that began with Willy Brandt and *Ostpolitik*. The Bonn Republic was overshadowed by the Cold War and the Nazi past, which in different ways constrained West German foreign policy during this period.

In Chapters 3 to 5, I examine the evolution of German foreign policy since reunification in 1990, which, I argue, should be understood in the context of the fault lines that had developed during the previous forty years. I argue that as the constraints that West Germany had faced disappeared, the Federal Republic underwent a mixture of continuity and change as the reunited Germany rethought its national identity and struggled with its relationship with the Nazi past. As Germany came under greater pressure to contribute to solving global problems, and in particular to modify its attitude to the use of military force, its foreign policy evolved in complex and sometimes unexpected ways. In particular, this evolution was informed by a competition between collective memories of Germans as perpetrators and as victims. I argue that, as the German economy became more dependent on exports in the 2000s, German foreign policy became more realist.

In Chapter 6, I examine developments since the euro crisis began in 2010, which, I argue, can be largely explained by the transformation in German national identity and the German economy that took place in the two decades between reunification and the outbreak of the crisis. The crisis thrust Germany into an extraordinary position of power, which allowed it to a large extent to impose its preferences on the rest of Europe. But rather than creating stability, its approach to the crisis has created instability in Europe. Moreover, while it has become economically assertive within Europe, it remains strikingly unassertive beyond Europe, where it has few of the aspirations of France and the UK to project power. Germany is once again a paradox.

I conclude that the "German question" has re-emerged in a new form. Once again, it is defined by a complex interaction between structural and ideological factors. Within the context of the EU, Germany's economy is too big for any of its neighbours, such as France, to challenge. But Germany is not, as some have argued, a European hegemon—nor can it be one. Rather, it has reverted to something like the position of "semi-hegemony" it had in Europe between 1871 and 1945—but in "geo-economic" rather than geopolitical form. At the same time, there has emerged a new form of German nationalism, which is based on exports and the idea of "peace", and a renewed sense of a "German mission"—which also reopens questions about Germany's relationship with the West.

1

THE GERMAN QUESTION

The unification of Germany transformed Europe. With the spectacular defeat of France and the proclamation of a united German *Reich* in the Hall of Mirrors in Versailles in January 1871, a new colossus in the centre of Europe had emerged. The historian Brendan Simms writes that "Where there had for hundreds of years been a plethora of smaller states, and as recently as seven years previously there had still been nearly forty distinct entities, a single power ruled supreme."[1] German power and French weakness upset the European equilibrium that had existed since the end of the Napoleonic Wars and had maintained peace in Europe. The British prime minister Benjamin Disraeli famously told the House of Commons in February 1871 that the "German revolution" had created a "new world". "The balance of power has been entirely destroyed," he said.[2]

The balance of power as a system of international relations had emerged following the Treaty of Westphalia in 1648. It was based on the idea that the great powers would threaten each other sufficiently to maintain a kind of balance between them that would prevent a general war in Europe.[3] It, in turn, was linked to the idea of *raison d'état*, or the national interest, that became the guiding principle of European diplomacy in the century following 1648. Revolutionary France's refusal to be bound by the notion of balance led to the Napoleonic Wars. But following France's defeat in 1815 the balance system was restored and institutionalised in the so-called Congress System. A balance between the five great powers—Austria, France, Great Britain, Prussia and Russia—would now keep the peace.

One of the weaknesses of the European balance of power, however, was Germany. Prior to the Napoleonic Wars, there had been around 300 or so German-speaking states in the area that subsequently became Germany. Following the Napoleonic Wars they were consolidated into around thirty larger entities. But these German states were either too weak or too strong. Whenever they were weak and divided, it tempted its neighbours, especially France, into expansionism. During the Thirty Years' War, for example, Germany became a battlefield for other powers. On the other hand, the prospect of a strong, united Germany scared other great powers, and France in particular. Thus Germany was either a power centre or a power vacuum—but either way created instability in Europe.[4]

Even before unification, the other great powers in Europe had been alarmed by the rapid rise of Prussia under Chancellor Otto von Bismarck.[5] But the new *Reich* that was created under his leadership in 1871 was far more powerful than even Prussia had been. It united the North German Federation that had been created following the defeat of Austria in 1866 and the southern states of Baden, Bavaria and Württemberg, which until the Franco-Prussian war had had pro-French tendencies, and the annexed territories of Alsace and Lorraine. The new Germany had a population of 41 million people, which was larger than France (36 million), Austria-Hungary (35.8) and Great Britain (31)—though still smaller than Russia (77)—and was increasing.[6] It also had a cutting-edge industrial economy that was growing rapidly, the best education system in the world and a formidable army.[7]

But despite these impressive resources, not even the new Germany was yet big or powerful enough to impose its will on Europe. Even though it had just won three wars in quick succession, it could not defeat a coalition of two or more of the other great powers. Thus the unified Germany was too big for a balance of power in Europe and too small for hegemony. The German historian Ludwig Dehio would later aptly identify Germany's problematic position in continental Europe during the *Kaiserreich* as one of "semi-hegemony": it was not powerful enough to impose its will on the continent; but at the same time it was powerful enough to be perceived as a threat by other powers.[8] Thus its size and central location in Europe—the so-called *Mittellage*—made it inherently destabilising. This, in essence, was what became known as the "German question".

This structural problem increasingly encouraged other European states to form coalitions to balance against German power. That in turn created a fear in Germany of a coalition of great powers—the so-called *cauchemar des coalitions*, or nightmare of coalitions. This fear of *Einkreisung*, or encirclement, led Germany to take measures to protect itself against such a coalition. But these measures would inevitably threaten each of the powers individually and thus accelerate the formation of the coalition Germany feared. Thus began what Hans-Peter Schwarz has called a "dialectic of encirclement".[9] Henry Kissinger writes that once Germany was transformed from a potential victim of aggression to a threat to the European equilibrium, "self-fulfilling prophecies became a part of the international system."[10]

Bismarck's immediate response to this structural problem after he became chancellor in 1871 was to dramatically change course. Until unification, he had pursued an expansionist foreign policy. But, haunted by the *cauchemar des coalitions*, he now sought to assuage fears of German power elsewhere in Europe—and thus to decrease the chances that other powers might seek to balance against Germany. He declared Germany to be a "satiated" power that had no further territorial ambitions. In particular, he sought to reassure Russia that Germany had no interest in the Balkans. This was the significance of his famous declaration that the whole of Balkans were not worth the healthy bones of a single Pomeranian grenadier.[11] In short, while Prussia had been a revisionist power, Germany now became a status quo power.

In search of security, Bismarck created an intricate system of overlapping alliances with other great powers in Europe. The key, he thought, was to avoid isolation. "All politics reduce themselves to this formula: to try to be one of three, as long as the world is governed by an unstable equilibrium of five Powers," he said in 1880.[12] Since reconciliation with France was impossible, above all because of the annexation of Alsace and Lorraine, he instead sought an alliance with the conservative powers Austria-Hungary and Russia—the so-called *Dreikaiserbund*, or Three Emperors' League, signed in 1873. When this alliance collapsed in the 1880s because of rivalry between Austria-Hungary and Russia in southeastern Europe, he signed two new secret treaties: the Triple Alliance with Austria and Italy, which guaranteed Germany allies in a war against France; and the Reinsurance Treaty with Russia, which ensured both countries' neutrality in the event that either went to war with another power. By 1882, Berlin was "the diplomatic capital of Europe".[13]

However, though in some ways brilliant, Bismarck's system of alliances was also fragile and, ultimately, disastrous: it was so elaborate that it required a statesman of his agility and creativity to maintain and manage it. In fact, even before Bismarck was forced out of office in 1890, it was already on the point of collapse.[14] It also presupposed that statesmen still had the almost complete freedom of manoeuvre that they had at the time of Metternich. In fact, however, by the second half of the nineteenth century, they were increasingly constrained by other forces. Although, as chancellor, Bismarck answered only to the Kaiser—who retained full power over foreign policy through what was known as *Kommandogewalt*, or the royal power of command—his success depended on being able to play off against each other the interests of various powerful forces that had to various degrees and in various ways made his unification through "blood and iron" possible.

First, Bismarck was under increasing pressure from, and had to make concessions to, the *Junker*—the conservative Prussian landowning class to which Bismarck himself belonged and to whom he owed his rise. The *Junker* opposed political liberalism and put pressure on Bismarck to resist greater democracy and to protect their own agricultural interests against increasing American and Russian competition. Second, Bismarck faced pressure from big business. In the decade following unification—the so-called *Gründerzeit*—a series of vast industrial corporations such as AEG and Siemens had emerged, which demanded access to resources and markets in order to expand, and, after the financial crash of 1873, protection in the form of tariffs. Third, the military exerted a significant influence on German foreign policy. In particular, the army and later the navy needed external threats in order to justify military spending.

Perhaps as important in a period in which public opinion mattered—what Simms has called an era of "popular geopolitics"—was nationalism.[15] German nationalism had emerged in the early nineteenth century when many of the hundreds of states that later cohered into a nation-state were under French occupation during the Napoleonic Wars. Broadly speaking, it included two currents that diverged in their relationship to the Enlightenment and the French Revolution. One was a liberal nationalist current, which aimed to apply the principles of the French revolution to Germany and to unify the patchwork of German states into a democratic, representative nation-state somewhat analogous to the French republic. The other was a romantic nationalist current, which sought to create a sense of German identity defined against the principles of the French revolution and more broadly against the Enlightenment.

German nationalism had begun as a progressive movement in opposition to the feudal-absolutist order in many of the German states. But after the revolution of 1848 failed—"German history reached its turning-point and failed to turn," A.J.P. Taylor famously wrote—this liberal nationalism was increasingly eclipsed by romantic nationalism.[16] Since there was during this period still no unified German nation-state around which a civic nationalism along French lines could cohere, German nationalism tended to attribute greater significance to culture in defining the nation than other European nationalisms. Under the influence of Herder and Fichte, it tended to centre on a romantic concept of the German nation based on a distinctively German *Volksgeist*, or national spirit, rooted in particular in the German language.

This romantic nationalism tended to define Germany in opposition to the West. In the second half of the nineteenth century, German nationalists increasingly defined German *Kultur* against French, or sometimes Western, *Zivilisation*. There was, as Michael Hughes has put it, an "intellectual rejection by some German nationalists of Western ideas and models and the search for a specifically 'German Way' in ideas, politics and social organisation" that was different from, and superior to, Western ways.[17] In particular, German nationalists rejected political liberalism as it had developed in Western nation states such as Britain, France and the United States. Thus a sense of German exceptionalism became central to German nationalism.

After unification, there was a triumphalist mood in Germany. Writing in 1873, Nietzsche saw a pernicious tendency in Germany to think that "German culture [had] also won a victory" in the conflict with France—in other words a sense of cultural rather than just technical superiority.[18] Germany represented a specific, unique combination of political, economic, military and educational institutions and based on "spiritual" rather than merely "materialist" values. German nationalists were especially dismissive of Britain and America, which they associated with liberalism and crass materialism—the nationalist historian Heinrich von Treitschke famously quipped that England had confused soap and civilisation. After the financial crash of 1873, German nationalism was also increasingly anti-Semitic as Jews were identified with liberalism and capitalism.

At the same time, this nationalism based on an idea of German exceptionalism included the idea that German culture should, in some as yet unspecified way, find global expression. In particular, nationalists imagined that, in realising its own identity, Germany would not just liberate itself but also redeem the whole world—especially the world beyond the West. This sense of a historic German mission was most memorably expressed in the words of the 1861 poem by Emanuel Geibel, "Deutschlands Beruf" ("Germany's mission"):

> Und es mag am deutschen Wesen
> Einmal noch die Welt genesen.
> (The essence of the German nation
> Will one day be the world's salvation).[19]

This idea of a German mission informed the emergence from the 1880s onwards of what Geoff Eley has called "empire talk".[20] Although Germany already called itself a *Reich*, or empire, some began to argue that it now needed greater territory. The argument was based on the idea that Germany's prosperity and even survival in the coming twentieth century, which would be dominated by continent-sized powers, depended on acquiring the resources it needed to become what some, such the writer Paul Rohrbach, called a "world empire" that could compete with Britain, Russia and the United States.[21] But unlike the other three empires, Germany was surrounded on all sides by great powers that would seek to prevent its expansion—what David Calleo has called its "continental straitjacket".[22] In other words, although from the outside Germany seemed powerful and threatening, many Germans saw it as weak and vulnerable.

There were two versions of this demand for a German empire. Some believed in *Mitteleuropa*: what Eley calls the idea of a "grand project of continental integration under German hegemony". They believed in further expansion *within* Europe rather than beyond it. However, others such as Bernhard von Bülow, the chancellor from 1900 to 1909, thought Germany should seek a "place in the sun"—that is, the empire in Africa and Asia—to which it, like other European great powers, was entitled. Thus there emerged in the late nineteenth century a tension between *Europapolitik* and *Weltpolitik*. In the decades from the 1880s to 1914 what Eley calls a "complex conversation" took place between these two competing ideas of empire by land and empire by sea.[23]

The demand for an overseas empire was driven in part by the needs of German corporations, which since the 1850s had sought concessions in Africa and Asia. Lobby groups such as the Kolonialverein (Colonial Union) and the Gesellschaft für deutsche Kolonisation (Society for German Colonisation), financed by big banks and industrialists, emerged to pressure the government into overseas expansion. But it was also driven in part by pressure from German nationalists who felt their country was being unfairly excluded from new markets and resources as the "scramble for Africa" was getting underway in the 1880s. Some even thought Germany's survival was at stake. In 1884 Heinrich von Treitschke said that colonisation was "eine Daseinsfrage", or "a matter of life and death".[24] In other words, the demand for an overseas empire was driven by both economic and geopolitical logic.

For Bismarck, Germany's destiny was within Europe. In 1888, Eugen Wolf, a proponent of a German empire in Africa, is supposed to have showed Bismarck a map of the continent and indicated where he thought Germany might acquire territory. "Your map of Africa is very nice", Bismarck is said to have replied. "But my map of Africa lies here in Europe. Here is Russia and here is France and here we are in the middle. That is my map of Africa."[25] Bismarck seems to have wanted to avoid antagonising other great powers such as Britain and France through an attempt at overseas expansion. At the same time, he thought they could be distracted, weakened or divided by their colonial adventures. Thus he had initially, in the words of one interlocutor, "refused all talk of colonies".[26]

However, with Germany in a depression in the early 1880s, Bismarck came under increasing pressure to make concessions to the colonialist lobby, which was demanding an all-out effort to acquire new markets as growth slowed. The historian Gordon Craig argues that Bismarck was impressed by the popular enthusiasm for colonisation and tried to exploit it. Hans-Ulrich Wehler, on the other hand, famously argued that Bismarck used colonial acquisition to resolve internal tensions within the *Reich*: what he called "social imperialism".[27] Whatever the explanation, in 1884 Bismarck took what Craig calls a "leap outwards into the world".[28] The acquisition of Angra-Paqueña in southern Namibia was followed by further territories in Togo and Cameroon in West Africa and New Guinea in the Pacific.

However, Bismarck's policy of pragmatic colonisation was nothing compared to what was to come when Wilhelm II came to the throne at the age of twenty-nine in 1888. After Bismarck resigned as chancellor in 1890, the Kaiser began to pursue a new course in foreign policy as he sought to make the *Reich* a "world empire". In January 1896 he proclaimed a new *Weltpolitik*. Following the murder of two German missionaries, the German navy seized the harbour of Kiaochow in China, alienating Russia in the process (this is when Bülow made his famous demand for a "place in the sun"). While Germany attempted to secure its position in central Europe, particularly through the new chancellor Leo von Caprivi's attempt to create a liberal European trading bloc, the emphasis was on "world policy" rather than "continental policy".

This new *Weltpolitik* "entranced" many Germans.[29] In 1898, the Kaiser was even approached by the Zionist leader Theodor Herzl, who tried to persuade him to support his idea of a Jewish state in Palestine—at the time part of the Ottoman Empire. Herzl, who in his novel *Altneuland* had imagined a kind of German Utopia in Palestine, told him he envisioned the Jewish state as a German protectorate that would export German culture to the Orient. Though the Kaiser did not ultimately support it, the idea seems initially to have appealed to him because it fitted in with his existing plans. In particular, he was seeking a concession to build a railway from Berlin to Constantinople—the first stretch of what became known as the Berlin-Baghdad railway—that would extend German influence through the Balkans and into the Middle East to fill the vacuum left by the ailing Ottoman Empire.[30]

Among the supporters of empire was Max Weber, who famously declared in his inaugural lecture in Freiburg in 1895 that unification would have amounted to no more than a "youthful prank" if Germany did not use it to become a *Weltmacht*, or world power.[31] "Liberal imperialists" such as Weber saw a German empire as a progressive cause and, as Ludwig Dehio puts it, aimed "not only to win a place in the sun for themselves but also to assure a brighter existence for others."[32] In particular, they saw it as Germany's mission to challenge British global hegemony. By challenging British sea power, Germany would create a global version of the balance of power that existed in Europe. Thus, Dehio suggests, "each of the rivals was fighting against the position of hegemony occupied by the other and appealing for a balance of power, but each attached a totally different meaning to the terms 'hegemony' and 'balance of power'."[33]

However, Brendan Simms argues, the "global turn in German grand strategy" at the end of the nineteenth century can also be seen not as a bid for power beyond Europe, but "a cry for help in Europe".[34] The Kaiser, who felt increasingly threatened by France in the west and Russia in the east, wanted an alliance—not conflict—with Britain, the only uncommitted European power, which would once again make Germany one of three in a Europe of five and in particular provide an ally against France. But especially after a dispute with Britain over the Transvaal in 1884–5, he was convinced that Britain would take Germany seriously only if it possessed a navy that, according to the "navalist" thinking of the time, would give it global clout. Thus he attempted to turn Germany, traditionally a land power, into a sea power. This was a second break with the approach of Bismarck, who in 1873 had told the British ambassador in Berlin that he "neither desired Colonies or Fleets for Germany".[35]

After the appointment of Admiral Alfred von Tirpitz as secretary of state for the navy in 1897, Germany began a huge naval build-up. Tirpitz, who had played a key role in the acquisition of Kiachow and was convinced that Britain was resolved to stop Germany fulfilling its destiny as a world power, told the Kaiser in a memo in 1897 that Germany needed "a certain measure of naval force as a political power factor" against Britain and should therefore produce "battleships in as great a number as possible".[36] The following year, the Reichstag passed the first of a series of five naval laws, which allocated 400 million reichsmarks for the construction of new ships. The chancellor, Prince Chlodwig Hohenlohe-Schillingsfürst, assured the Reichstag that "a policy of adventure is far from our minds."[37] But the effect of the policy was inevitably to start an arms a race with Britain, which was more dependent on overseas trade than any other great power and sought to maintain a fleet powerful enough to defeat two continental powers at sea—the so-called two-power standard.

Meanwhile, the geopolitical map of Europe was also changing—in part as a response to German power and in part as a consequence of shifts in the complex mixture of competition and co-operation between the great powers beyond Europe. French foreign policy continued to focus above all on containing Germany. Since German unification, Austria had shifted its foreign policy focus from central to south-eastern Europe, where, however, it came into increasing conflict with Russia. Meanwhile, Germany had in 1890 allowed the Reinsurance Treaty with Russia to lapse, while it remained committed to the alliance with Austria-Hungary and Italy. In the early 1890s, a rapprochement between France and

Russia took place—the beginning of what George Kennan would later call "the fateful alliance".[38] Thus what in 1871 had been a multipolar system of five powers turned gradually into a bipolar system of two competing alliance blocs.

As it became increasingly overstretched around the world, Britain's attitude to alliances also changed. In 1904, Britain and France signed the Entente Cordiale, which put an end to their rivalry in North Africa and ended Britain's long tradition of "splendid isolation". Germany sought to divide Britain and France by challenging a French attempt to consolidate control over Morocco in 1905, but instead found itself isolated at the subsequent Algeciras Conference. Many in the British foreign-policy establishment who had until then focused on tensions with France and Russia reached the conclusion that the biggest threat was now Germany, which sought a form of maritime supremacy that was "incompatible with the existence of the British empire", as a British diplomat, Eyre Crowe, put it in a famous memorandum in 1907.[39] The same year, Britain and Russia signed a convention that completed the coalescence of an Anglo-French-Russian bloc—the Triple Entente.

In 1906 Britain had responded to German naval expansion by concentrating on the construction of a new type of battleship, the Dreadnought, which would be superior in terms of armour and mobility to any existing battleship. In 1908 Germany itself responded by replacing older ships with dreadnought-type battleships. After becoming chancellor in 1909, Theobald von Bethmann-Hollweg tried, but failed, to end the naval arms race. In 1911 the dispatch by Germany of the gunboat *Panther* to the Moroccan port of Agadir in response to the dispatch of French troops to Fez to put down unrest caused a second Moroccan crisis. The "Panther's leap" further increased tension between Germany and the Triple Entente, accelerated the arms race and created a widespread sense in Europe that war was inevitable. In 1913 the German army was massively expanded and some in the military command, including Chief of Staff Helmuth von Moltke, began to call for "preventive war".

Thus, whether as the direct consequence of German policy or the indirect "European consequence of world-historical transitions", as Christopher Clark has recently argued, the *cauchemar des coalitions* became a reality.[40] When war finally broke out in August 1914, the catalyst was the strategic competition between Austria-Hungary and Russia in the Balkans rather than between Britain and Germany—the eastern question rather than the German question. But the bipolar system of competing blocs turned a conflict between Austria and Russia into a general European war. As Germany made a bid for hegemony in Europe forty-three years after unification, it continued to be informed by the idea of a German mission. When the German intelligentsia went to war, it was, as David Blackbourn has put it, "the supposedly superior depth of its culture that it brandished against the enemy."[41]

After World War I, Germany was diminished but not destroyed. The Treaty of Versailles, signed in 1919 in the same place where German unification had been proclaimed in 1871, imposed punitive terms on Germany that limited its resources and freedom of manoeuvre. As well as having to sign a war guilt clause and pay reparations of $64 billion, Germany lost significant territory, including Alsace-Lorraine to France and Pomerania and parts of East Prussia and Silesia to Poland, and all of the colonies beyond Europe that it had acquired since Bismarck. In addition, the Saar region was placed under French control and the Rhineland was to be demilitarised and occupied for fifteen years. Restrictions were also placed on the German military: its army was limited to 100,000 men; it could have no tanks or heavy artillery or even a general staff; and its navy could have no large ships or submarines.

However, although Germany was significantly weaker and faced greater constraints than before World War I, the basic configuration of Europe remained unchanged. Peace depended, as it had before the war, on the balance of power. In particular, in the centre of Europe, the "German question" remained unresolved. In relative terms, Germany was actually more powerful than it was before because other empires had collapsed and France was drained. Around it, the belt of small nation states created out of former European empires that was meant to function as a buffer instead exacerbated instability in Europe. A first attempt was made at a new approach of collective security through the creation of the League of Nations, but it was not yet backed by military power. The punitive terms of the Treaty of Versailles created resentment in Germany: before the war French revisionism had been a threat to equilibrium; now German revisionism was.

The objective of German diplomacy in what became the Weimar Republic was above all to recover independence and sovereignty. In particular, it sought to reduce and eventually eliminate altogether the punitive reparations payments that had been imposed on Germany by the

Versailles Treaty, to agree the withdrawal of foreign troops from Germany, to attain military parity with the other powers, and finally, if possible, to recover territory lost to Poland. These objectives were shared by most of the political class in Germany. Meanwhile the rest of Europe was divided and conflicted: France between seeking to delay the recovery of Germany and reconciliation with it; Britain between its traditional role as offshore balancer and its commitment to the new idea of collective security.

Excluded from the League of Nations and ostracised by the Western powers, Germany and the Soviet Union in 1922 signed the Rapallo Treaty, in which they established full diplomatic relations and renounced claims against each other. In response, in 1923 French and Belgian troops occupied the Ruhr, Germany's industrial heartland. Over the following months, Berlin sponsored a campaign of passive resistance against the occupation and Germany descended into hyperinflation and political disorder as the government printed money to pay war reparations. "If there had been no Rapallo, there would have been no Ruhr," Lloyd George would later say.[42] Although the economy was stabilised the following year, the hyperinflation of 1923 left behind a trauma and the occupation had changed German strategic thinking.

The situation was stabilised by the National Liberal Gustav Stresemann, who was foreign minister from 1924 until his death from a stroke in 1929. Stresemann had been an early advocate of the importance of economics as a factor in international relations and believed the rise of the United States would change the European balance of power. The war shook Stresemann's faith in the use of military force as a means of power politics. Thus although he was a "full-blooded German nationalist" who sought to revise the terms of the Treaty of Versailles and the restrictions placed upon Germany, and ultimately to recover territory lost to Poland, he sought to use economic rather than military means to achieve Germany's foreign-policy objectives—what Adam Tooze has called "economic revisionism" and Gottfried Niedhart an "economic version of German power politics".[43]

It was brilliantly successful. By indicating a willingness to fulfil the reparations terms, Stresemann gained US support in the form of loans and exploited the differences between Britain and France to win concessions on reparations. In 1924 the Dawes Plan substantially reduced the immediate reparation demands on Germany and facilitated a $100 million loan from American lenders. In 1925 the Locarno Treaties guaranteed the removal of British and French troops from the Ruhr and allowed Germany to join the League of Nations in exchange for the recognition of Germany's western borders. The occupation of the Rhineland was ended in 1928 and further reductions in reparations were agreed in the Young Plan in 1929. But while Germany had achieved many of its foreign-policy objectives through co-operation rather than confrontation by the end of the 1930s, the mainstream parties were increasingly undermined by radical nationalist parties such as the Nazis—particularly following the Wall Street Crash in 1929 and the ensuing depression.

After Hitler became chancellor in 1933, Germany became more aggressively revisionist than it had previously been. Rather than "meekly accepting a place for Germany within a global economic order dominated by the affluent English-speaking countries", Hitler sought to "mount an epic challenge to this order", writes Tooze.[44] Hitler initially focused on lifting the remaining restrictions on Germany, but unlike his predecessors he took unilateral action and was prepared to use military force: in autumn 1933 Germany left the League of Nations and refused to abide by the arms limitations imposed on it by Versailles; in 1935 the Saar was returned to Germany following a plebiscite; in 1936 Germany sent troops into the demilitarised Rhineland. Hitler also geared the economy for war and openly rearmed and expanded the size of the military beyond the limits set by Versailles. By 1939, Germany was powerful enough to once again seek hegemony in Europe.[45]

With the beginning of World War II, both Nazi ideology and strategy were radicalised even further. Hitler initially sought to avoid the mistakes of World War I by avoiding fighting a war on two fronts simultaneously. Thus in 1939 he agreed the Nazi-Soviet Pact—a version of Rapallo between two totalitarian states. However, the war in the west did not come to an end as quickly as Hitler had hoped. In the summer of 1941, compelled by both ideology and the need for resources, Hitler invaded the Soviet Union and in doing so created precisely the two-front war German foreign policy had always sought to avoid. After the invasion of the Soviet Union, expansion in central and Eastern Europe evolved into a genocidal project of economic exploitation and the extermination of populations to create *Lebensraum* for the German people.

In what became the largest, most brutal, and most ambitious reshaping of Europe in history, the Nazis reactivated, radicalised and realised the idea of a continental empire that went back to the "empire talk" of the 1880s. As Mark Mazower has shown, the Nazis aimed to transpose elements of other extra-European imperial projects such as the British Empire, and of their own colonial experiments in Africa and the Far East, onto the European continent.[46] Thus it was a reversion, albeit in extreme form, to the idea of an empire by land, rather than by sea, that Bismarck had sought. In fact, like Bismarck, Hitler described Russia as "our Africa".[47] At the same time, the Nazis sometimes couched this imperial project in the rhetoric of an *europäische Gemeinschaft*, or "European community".

This imperial project reached its high point in 1943. After the defeat at Stalingrad Germany was in retreat but fought on; by 1945, it was completely destroyed—unlike in 1918. Germany—and Europe—would never be the same again. The "German question" that had caused instability since unification had, after the destruction of much of the continent, transformed the role of Europe in the world. Following World War II, two external superpowers displaced the pre-war great powers in Europe. A new fault line went through Europe—and through Germany. The German question would, therefore, be resolved by the division of Europe and by American and Soviet power. As A.J.P Taylor put it, "what had been the centre of the world became merely the 'European question'."[48]

Thus German foreign policy between 1871 and 1945 was informed by a complex interaction between structural factors and what might be called ideological factors—what David Calleo has called "the inner compulsions of German society".[49] After World War II, historians and sociologists argued that Germany had undergone a kind of *Fehlentwicklung*, or misdevelopment, that culminated in Nazism. This was the idea of a German *Sonderweg*, or "special path". The term originally referred to the historiographical theory of Germany's aberrant historical trajectory, which diverged from that of France and the United Kingdom, but has also been used more generally to refer to German exceptionalism in both negative and positive connotations.

The term *Sonderweg* had originally been used in a positive sense since the beginning of the nineteenth century to refer to the German perception of difference from the West. The idea of the *Sonderweg* then reappeared in negative form in 1960s. Influenced by Marx and Weber, some, such as the sociologist Ralf Dahrendorf and the historian Hans-Ulrich Wehler, sought now to use the term as a way to understand the German catastrophe rather than the German genius. The idea that Germany was in some sense an "abnormal" nation state was in turn linked to Helmuth Plessner's idea of Germany as a *verspätete Nation*, or "belated nation", and its perceived consequences. Different versions of the *Sonderweg* thesis place different emphases on the *Mittellage*; the influence of Prussian militarism; German intellectual history and in particular its aberrations from Enlightenment ideas, irrationalism and inwardness; and the nature of German society, in particular the role of the bourgeoisie.

One particularly influential version of the *Sonderweg* thesis saw the explanation of Germany's fatefully aberrant trajectory in the failure of the 1848 revolution in Germany. The argument was that, because Germany had no bourgeois revolution like that of 1688 in England or 1789 in France, the German bourgeoisie was weak or underdeveloped, and failed during the nineteenth century to constitute itself as a self-conscious class-subject acting politically in its own collective interests—that is, in direct confrontation with the established domination of the landowning aristocracy. Instead, 1848 was followed by a "re-feudalisation" of the bourgeoisie. Some argued that this *Fehlentwicklung* was also a cause of German expansionism. Wehler argued that Bismarck and his successors used colonial acquisition to resolve internal tensions within the *Reich*—what he called "social imperialism".[50]

The *Sonderweg* thesis is now less widely accepted than it used to be. In a groundbreaking study published in 1980, David Blackbourn and Geoff Eley showed that the idea of *Fehlentwicklung* was misleading in several ways: it idealised American, English or French history; it oversimplified the role of bourgeoisie in Germany; and it assumed bourgeois revolution led to liberalism.[51] But more recently, Helmut Walser Smith has argued that the "anti-*Sonderweg* consensus" that followed has undermined any sense of the "deep continuities" in German history.[52] In particular, Walser Smith argues that it underplays nationalism and anti-Semitism as "causal streams" and cuts off most of the nineteenth century before 1890 from the twentieth-century "German catastrophe".[53]

While historians and sociologists have tended to focus on domestic factors, international relations theorists have tended to explain German expansionism by reference either to the nature of states in general or the anarchic nature of the international system. German unification had created a paradigmatic case of what realists call the "security dilemma": in search of security in an anarchic international system, states follow policies that increase their own military capabilities; but in doing so, they inadvertently make other states feel less secure; this creates a vicious circle or spiral to which there is no permanent or lasting solution. So-called defensive realists such as Kenneth Waltz argue that states seek to maintain the balance of power—that is, the status quo. But although Bismarck's foreign policy after 1871 offers some support for this theory, it does not explain the increasingly expansionist foreign policy Germany pursued after Bismarck resigned.

So-called offensive realists such as John Mearsheimer, on the other hand, argue that states seek to maximise their own power rather than to maintain equilibrium. According to this view, "there are no status quo powers in the international system, save for the occasional hegemon that wants to maintain its dominating position over potential rivals."[54] Mearsheimer argues that German foreign policy from 1871 to 1945 is therefore a "straightforward" case of a great power acting as an offensive realist power.[55] He argues that both the Kaiser and Hitler made a bid for hegemony in Europe when they were able to—in other words when Germany became relatively powerful enough. Thus in foreign-policy terms, "Hitler did not represent a sharp break with the past but instead thought and behaved like German leaders before him."[56] In other words, it was, like the version told by historians and sociologists who put forward the idea of a German *Sonderweg*, a story of continuity.

As illustrated by the different conclusions that historians, sociologists and international relations theorists have reached about the continuity in German history, and about Germany's role in pre-1945 international relations in Europe, there is still no interdisciplinary consensus about the "German question". What is clear is that German unification in 1871 created a new central power in Europe, which pursued an expansionist foreign policy that ultimately led to catastrophe. What remains in dispute is the extent to which the ultimate causes were structural or ideological—in other words whether they were a function of the nature of states or of a specific set of ideas prevalent in Germany. But until recently, this had seemed like a purely academic question: the German question seemed, as David Calleo put it in 1978, "to have passed into history".[57]

2

IDEALISM AND REALISM

The Federal Republic was the legal successor to the Third Reich and many of the men who ran the country in the decade after its creation in 1949 were former Nazis. We now know that the continuities between the Third Reich and the newly formed republic were particularly strong in the case of the foreign ministry. A few years ago a team of four historians went through the foreign ministry's files and wrote an exhaustive history of its relationship with the Nazis and its engagement with the Nazi past following the end of the war. They not only confirmed the foreign ministry's complicity in the Holocaust but also showed how many diplomats implicated in it had resumed their careers after the war. In fact, they found, there were actually more Nazis in the ministry in the 1950s than during the Nazi era itself.[1]

However, although 1945 was not the "hour zero" that many in Germany would later imagine it was, it was nevertheless a break—at least in foreign policy. Although some of the officials in the foreign ministry were the same men who had implemented Hitler's foreign policy, the Federal Republic that was created in 1949 was not the Third Reich—though in the 1960s some young left-wing West Germans would claim it was.[2] Not only was the country devastated by the war, it was also about half the size of the Germany that had declared war in 1939, and had lost important resources such as coal. It would also become a democracy with an economy that the Western allies had transformed—in particular by breaking up the cartels that had dominated the German economy since the *Gründerzeit*. The devastation of 1945 had also changed the German people. In particular, their attitude to war had been transformed.

Germany's environment was also totally changed by the emergence of the Cold War, with which the creation of the Federal Republic coincided—and in which it was itself a factor. From unification in 1871 until the catastrophe of 1945, Germany had been a powerful state in the centre of Europe; the Federal Republic, on the other hand, was a weak state on the eastern edge of western Europe. In other words, it had in a sense gone from *Mittellage* to *Grenzlage*—from the centre to the edge. The enclave of West Berlin was more vulnerable still—as the Soviet blockade of 1948/9 dramatically illustrated. This meant that, for most of its life, West Germany operated under unusual constraints. Until reunification in 1990, it was a "semi-sovereign state, dependent on its allies for protection against the Soviet threat and inhibited by the history of the Second World War from defining or explicitly pursuing its own national interests."[3]

Within these constraints, the Federal Republic pursued two foreign-policy goals above all: security and rehabilitation. For much of the history of the Federal Republic, its security was precarious. In fact, such has been the importance of security to West Germany that some historians have told its whole story as a search for security.[4] Rehabilitation was a softer objective but nevertheless an important one because success in achieving it could increase freedom of manoeuvre. The Federal Republic was in a limited sense revisionist: the pre-amble of the Basic Law committed it to reunification. But this was gradually downgraded as a foreign-policy objective and was increasingly seen as a long-term goal that was dependent upon a wider transformation of Europe.

In its pursuit of the two objectives of rehabilitation and security in this unusual situation, the Federal Republic evolved what to many seemed to be a new approach to foreign policy—one, in fact, that was quite the opposite of the foreign policy Germany had pursued between 1871 and 1945. It was based on the idea of international integration in multilateralist institutions—in particular NATO and what became the European Union. This approach, which evolved gradually during the forty-year history of the Federal Republic, led some to see it as an entirely new kind of foreign-policy actor. It was not a realist great power like its legal predecessor, but a normative power—in other words, one that set international norms.[5] Perhaps most importantly, in a context in which collective security replaced the balance of power, West Germany rejected the use of military force except in self-defence.

Perhaps the most influential way to understand this new approach to foreign policy was the idea that the Federal Republic was a "civilian power"—that is, one that, unlike a great power, aims to "civilise" international relations by strengthening international norms. The term, which is both descriptive and prescriptive, was coined by François Duchêne in the early 1970s to describe the European Union. It was applied to Germany by Hanns Maull, who argued that Germany, along with Japan, had become a "prototype" of "a new type of international power" that accepted the necessity of co-operation with others in the pursuit of international objectives, concentrated on non-military and, in particular, economic means to achieve its foreign-policy goals, and was willing to transfer sovereignty to supranational institutions.[6]

Maull argued that Germany and Japan had become "civilian powers" largely by necessity rather than choice. Defeated in World War II, they were forced to make territorial concessions. But, because of the emergence of the Cold War, it was not in their national interest to make any territorial demands: to do so would have undermined their own stability. In the context of the Cold War, they also both renounced an autonomous security policy in favour of strategic dependence on the United States—a relatively cheap and effective solution to their defence problems that allowed them to focus energy instead on economic growth. In short, the Federal Republic did not adopt a "civilian power" identity in an act of altruism. Rather, it did so because it saw it as the best way of achieving its own foreign-policy ambitions and objectives.

As Maull himself acknowledged, the concept of a "civilian power" was in many ways similar to that of the "trading state" that Richard Rosecrance had developed.[7] Rosecrance argued that, in the 1970s and 1980s, driven by the declining value of fixed productive assets, states for whom a traditional strategy was no longer feasible, either because of size or because of their recent experience with conflict, had increasingly adopted strategies based on augmenting their share of world trade rather than traditional military power or territorial expansion. As a result, there had emerged "a new political prototype" of states that sought their vocation through international commerce rather than territorial expansion. Other foreign-policy analysts have specifically applied the concept of a "trading state" to Germany.[8]

However, although "civilian powers" such as Germany were in practice often also "trading states", the former differ conceptually from the latter in terms of their ultimate objective. In particular, Maull's version of the concept of "civilian power" originates in the sociologist Norbert Elias's theory of the civilising process in politics and society.[9] For a "civilian power", the overriding foreign-policy objective is not simply to improve economic performance or prosperity but to civilise international relations through the development of the international rule of law. In other words, a "civilian power" aims to make international politics like domestic politics. In particular, by avoiding the use of force except collectively and with international legitimacy, it aims to contribute to the development of a multilateral monopoly on the use of force analogous to the state's monopoly on the use of force in a domestic context.

Maull emphasises that the idea of a "civilian power" is an ideal-typical one. The Federal Republic, together with Japan, may have come closer to realising this ideal than any other state. But the history of the Federal Republic is not a seamless one. In practice, foreign-policy decisions were made, as in other democratic states, through a complex interaction between actors representing various competing interests. There were also shifts over time in West German foreign policy. Useful as they are, accounts of Germany as a new "prototype" in international relations inevitably emphasise the consensus that has existed in German foreign policy and downplay the fault lines in German foreign-policy debates. In order to understand some of the shifts that took place after reunification in 1990, it is necessary to examine these fault lines in more detail.

Debates about US foreign policy tend to take place within the framework of the concepts of idealism and realism. According to Richard Haass, for example, "the battle between realists and idealists is the fundamental fault line of the American foreign-policy debate."[10] Idealism tends to be associated with an "ideological" US foreign policy involving the promotion of norms or values, and in particular democracy. Idealists tend to believe in US engagement with the world. Realism, on the other hand, tends to be associated with an "anti-ideological" US foreign policy involving the pursuit of harder national interests and, in particular, economic or strategic interests. Realism in US foreign policy tends to be associated with isolationism, but also with imperialism.

The foreign policy of the Federal Republic is rarely analysed as a competition between idealist and realist currents in this way. This is in part because of the great degree of consensus around the Federal Republic's foreign policy associated with the idea of "civilian power"—that is, an idealist approach that contrasts with the realist approach in German foreign policy before 1945. It is also in part because, in so far as differences existed in the Federal Republic, they have tended to be seen in left-right terms. However, it is possible to identify a tension between competing approaches in West German foreign-policy debates that cuts across the left-right divide. In fact, within the constraints of semi-sovereignty and the Cold War, two distinct currents in post-war West German foreign-policy thinking emerged before reunification in 1990: one realist and one idealist.

Walter Russell Mead has proposed an alternative approach to understanding US foreign policy based on "the questions and interests that actually drive the American foreign policy process".[11] Developing and complicating the contrast between idealism and realism in US foreign policy, he identifies four approaches, or schools, that began relatively early in the history of the United States and have remained identifiable up to the present day, though they have also evolved in responses to changes in the United States and in the international order, and have influenced American foreign policy. Each of the four, identified by Mead with a leading American politician (Jefferson, Hamilton, Jackson and Wilson), represents a distinct vision of America's identity and role in the world.

Although the history of the Federal Republic is much shorter than that of the United States, it is nevertheless possible to identify distinct approaches to foreign policy in an analogous way. According to Mead, the four schools of American foreign policy emerged as different responses to the challenges presented by the question of the relationship of the United States to the international order that, throughout most of its history, was centred on Great Britain. Of course, the Federal Republic has a different geography and history—and therefore different approaches based on different ideas. The fault lines in the Federal Republic's foreign-policy debates emerged in response to the specific challenges it faced during the Cold War. In particular, they centred on the Germany's relationship to the West and to the Nazi past. In other words, debates about German foreign policy have tended to take place on two axes: a geographical one and a historical one.

The main arguments in West German foreign policy until reunification centred on the nation and its relationship to the West. Security and rehabilitation—West Germany's two most important foreign-policy objectives—required international integration and in particular ties with the West—the so-called *Westbindung*. However, the development of such ties deepened the division of Germany. There was therefore a tension between West Germany's security and its relationship with East Germany. Thus two approaches to West German foreign policy emerged: one that sought to deepen the *Westbindung*, even at the cost of deepening the division of Germany; and another that emphasised unity above all and therefore rejected the *Westbindung* if it came at the expense of deepening the division.

In German history until 1945, nationalism had in general been identified with the right. The left, on the other hand, had tended to be internationalist. But in the Federal Republic from 1949 onwards, the centre-left was, in foreign-policy terms, more nationalist than the right. Against the background of the Cold War, the centre-right Christian Democrats, who were in power for the first twenty years of the Federal Republic, sought above all to integrate West Germany into the West. The centre-left Social Democrats, who were in opposition until 1966, challenged this approach and sought to keep open the possibility of German reunification. Thus the central fault line in West German foreign policy was between a centre-right idealism, which focused on the idea of "freedom", and a centre-left nationalism, which focused on the idea of "peace".

The first decisive figure in West German foreign policy was Konrad Adenauer, the former Christian Democrat mayor of Cologne, who became the first chancellor of the Federal Republic in 1949 and stayed in power until 1964. When Adenauer became chancellor, the Federal Republic was still a protectorate of the three Western allies—France, the United Kingdom and the United States. Under the Occupation Statute, the three countries' high commissioners retained the right to intervene if they thought it was necessary for security reasons or to uphold democratic government in West Germany. Adenauer's primary objective was therefore to achieve greater freedom of manoeuvre from the occupying powers while retaining their protection against the Soviet threat.

In some ways, Adenauer's approach was analogous to the one taken by Stresemann in the 1920s. Their strategies were both based on a recognition of German weakness. Like Stresemann, Adenauer aimed to increase his freedom of manouevre. But the situation in the late 1940s and early

1950s was quite different: in the context of Soviet power, in particular nuclear weapons, and the Cold War, security mandated not just US economic support as in the 1920s but also US military support. Adenauer's aim was therefore to turn the Federal Republic into an equal member of the Western alliance. Moreover, unlike Streseman, an Anglophobe *Vernunftrepublikaner* (that is, a republican by reason rather than conviction), Adenauer believed in an alliance of democracies that had "the same basic views on the meaning of life" and would "defend the common ideals of the free world against the Soviet threat".[12] Thus Adenauer's approach to foreign policy was an idealist one.

Adenauer's first success in this respect was the Petersberg Agreement of 1949, which both brought to an end the dismantling of West German industry and made the Federal Republic a member of the Ruhr Authority, from which it had until then been excluded—the first multilateral institution in which it was an equal partner. But the real breakthrough was the Schuman Plan of 1950, which the following year led to the creation of the European Coal and Steel Community (ECSC). The idea of integrating the coal and steel industries of France, Italy, the Benelux states and West Germany had been proposed by the French foreign minister, Robert Schuman, who hoped that pooling industrial production in this way would make war between France and Germany "not merely unthinkable, but materially impossible".[13]

The Schuman Plan is now remembered as the beginning of the process that culminated in the creation of the European Union, the single market and the single currency. At the time, however, its significance for the Federal Republic was more prosaic. The creation of the ECSC contributed to the rehabilitation of West Germany by integrating its economy into that of other western European states while creating economic opportunities and in particular guaranteeing German industry a new market. At the same time, however—and perhaps most importantly—it increased West German sovereignty. In particular, it created an important new multilateral institution in which the Federal Republic was an equal partner rather than a defeated country under occupation.[14]

Adenauer's approach was rejected by Kurt Schumacher, the leader of the Social Democrats, who had spent the war in concentration camps including Dachau. Schumacher remained committed to German reunification as a foreign-policy priority and accused Adenauer of selling Germany out. After Adenauer agreed to take part in—and therefore recognise—the Ruhr Authority, Schumacher called him "the chancellor of the Allies".[15] The Social Democrats also opposed the Schuman Plan, which they argued further undermined the possibility of Germany reunification and pulled the Federal Republic towards a bloc—the core of what would become the EU—that was conservative, clerical and capitalist.[16] Thus the pre-war situation in which the right had accused the left of a lack of patriotism had been reversed: now it was the left that was questioning the patriotism of the centre-right.

It wasn't that Adenauer was actually opposed to German reunification—though some speculated that, for political reasons, he was quite happy to lose the Social Democrat heartlands that now formed part of East Germany. But Adenauer thought reunification was only possible in a transformed Europe. Thus European integration offered a more promising way to pursue national interests than the pursuit of sovereignty. He therefore tended to emphasise security and rehabilitation at the expense of reunification. Reunification remained for Adenauer a long-term objective, but one that was subordinate to the more pressing objectives of increasing the Federal Republic's freedom of manoeuvre from the occupying powers and integration into the West. In 1952 Adenauer therefore rejected Stalin's offer of a united, neutral, unoccupied Germany.

The Korean War, which began in the summer of 1950 and drew US attention away from Europe towards Asia, had made West Germany even more vulnerable to the Soviet threat. Against this background, in the second half of the 1950s Adenauer took two steps to further integrate the Federal Republic into the West that also further deepened the division of Europe and helped stabilise the German Democratic Republic (GDR). First, in 1955, West Germany rearmed and joined NATO. This was an even more controversial step than the creation of the ECSC—not least because it militarised the German-German border and created the real possibility that West German soldiers might have to shoot at East German soldiers and vice versa. It was once again opposed by the Social Democrats, who favoured neutrality and opposed rearmament in the name of "peace".

The second step that completed the *Westbindung* was the Treaty of Rome in 1957, which created the European Economic Community and set a goal of "an ever closer union among the peoples of Europe". For West Germany, European integration was, as Stanley Hoffmann has put it, "a leap from opprobrium and impotence, to respectability and equal rights".[17] According to Timothy Garton Ash, West Germany had "a hard national interest in demonstrating ... European commitment, for only by regaining the trust of their neighbors and international partners (including the United States and the Soviet Union) could they achieve their long-term goal of German reunification." In other words, "West German Europeanism was not simply instrumental—it reflected a real moral and emotional engagement—but nor was it purely idealistic."[18]

Adenauer's centre-right idealist approach was brilliantly successful in securing and rehabilitating West Germany. But by the early 1960s, it had reached its limits. After the Berlin Wall was erected in the summer of 1961, the situation in Europe stabilised. In addition, the strategic situation had changed: the US no longer had supremacy in strategic nuclear weapons and the new US president, John F. Kennedy, had placed a new emphasis on peace. Meanwhile, at its Bad Godesberg conference in 1959, the Social Democrats had finally reconciled themselves to the *Westbindung*. It was from this new context that a fresh, distinctive approach to West German foreign policy—the first alternative to Adenauer's idealist approach—was to emerge. The intellectual driving force behind this new approach was West Berlin mayor Willy Brandt's adviser Egon Bahr. Henry Kissinger would later write that Brandt's policy, conceived by Bahr, "reversed" and "transcended" the foreign policy of the Federal Republic up to that point.[19]

Bahr, born in 1922, thought above all in national terms. He was an admirer of Kurt Schumacher and of the Christian Democrat Jakob Kaiser, who had described Adenauer as a "separatist".[20] Bahr wanted Germany to recover what he later called "inner sovereignty" and pursue its national interest more confidently. He thought Adenauer had misjudged the German national interest, which was not identical to that of the United States. Above all Adenauer had neglected reunification, which was incompatible with integration into the West. The Federal Republic's combination of integration with the West and rigid anti-communism had produced a fundamentally imbalanced foreign policy: "supranational to the West, demands to the East; a readiness to compromise towards the West, unyielding fundamental positions to the East".[21] Instead, Germany needed a plan for reunification.

At a retreat at Tutzing on Lake Starnberg in Bavaria in the summer of 1963, Bahr outlined the new approach to the German question. The conditions for reunification could only be achieved with the Soviet

Union, not against it. Logically, therefore, the Federal Republic should not seek to undermine the GDR regime but to stabilise it. It should accept the existence of the GDR and seek gradual improvements in living conditions for East Germans through foreign trade and the "weaving" of political, economic and cultural ties between West and East Germany. These ties would be transformative—what he called *Wandel durch Annäherung*, or "change through rapprochement"—and could lead to German reunification at the end of a series of "small steps". Bahr thought of it as "judo".[22] The East German foreign minister, meanwhile, called it "aggression in slippers".[23]

Bahr had a chance to implement the new approach after Brandt became the first Social Democrat chancellor of the Federal Republic in 1969—by which time there was a new international context. In 1968 Richard M. Nixon had succeeded Lyndon B. Johnson as US president. His national security adviser, Henry Kissinger, began a new policy of détente towards the Soviet Union and opened a back channel with Bahr, whom he had first met in Washington in 1964. Kissinger was initially worried by Bahr's proposed new approach to *Deutschlandpolitik*, which he thought came from an "essentially nationalist perspective".[24] After all, although it involved a pragmatic acceptance of the division of Germany, it was intended as a way to achieve German unity—albeit in the long term through a series of small steps. Although Washington was not opposed to German unity, it did not want it to happen at the cost of the "Finlandisation" of the Federal Republic.

Bahr's new approach was what Gordon Craig calls an "anti-ideological"—that is, a realist—one.[25] In fact, Kissinger saw Bahr in the tradition of Bismarck, who, like him, "sought to exploit Germany's central position for its national goals". Those goals were of course different in Bahr's day than in Bismarck's, but the thinking of Bahr nevertheless represented for Kissinger a return to the logic of the *Mittellage*. Bahr sought to maximise the Federal Republic's freedom of manoeuvre and actively distinguish its approach to Moscow from that of its superpower ally. Kissinger thought that Bahr, unlike Adenauer, lacked an emotional attachment to the Atlantic alliance. But his fear was not that West Germany would leave NATO, which it still needed for protection against the Soviet Union, but that it might "avoid controversies outside of Europe even when they affected fundamental security interests".[26]

For Kissinger and other Western leaders, "a free-wheeling, powerful Germany trying to maneuver between East and West, whatever its ideology, posed the classic challenge to the equilibrium of Europe."[27] In the context of the Cold War, Kissinger feared that *Ostpolitik* could in turn undermine transatlantic unity and play into the hands of Soviet Union, which could play Europe off against the United States as part of a strategy of "differential détente". "In some circumstances it might be in Europe's interest to separate itself from the United States so as to improve its freedom of maneuver toward the Soviet Union."[28] In particular, Europe might accommodate itself to Soviet power through closer economic relations that would increase Europe's dependence on the Soviet Union. Thus the rhetoric of peace and the reality of economic interdependence could undermine the West.

However, Kissinger came to think that "whatever the pitfalls of *Ostpolitik*, the alternative"—that is, opposing it and risking cutting West Germany loose from its Western allies and European partners—"was riskier still".[29] The US therefore supported Brandt as he signed a series of treaties with Eastern Bloc states starting in 1970. The new approach also helped to resolve a major American worry up to that point: West Berlin. By insisting on linking *Ostpolitik* with the issue, the US was able to extract concessions from the Soviet Union. As Kissinger later put it, "support for *Ostpolitik* gave America the leverage needed to end the twenty-year-old crisis over Berlin."[30] In 1971 a comprehensive agreement was reached that guaranteed the security of, and access to, the "front city". As Kissinger later wrote, "Berlin disappeared from the list of international crisis spots."[31]

Thus, though Kennedy's "peace strategy" had created the space for *Ostpolitik*, Bahr's policy of détente dovetailed neatly with that of Kissinger. Bahr would later write that he was grateful to Kissinger. "Without him there our détente policy would not have existed in this form," he said.[32] Despite the rhetoric of "peace", *Ostpolitik* should therefore be seen as a realist strategy—that is, one that centred on the concepts of the national interest and the balance of power that went back to Richelieu. In his book on *Ostpolitik*, *In Europe's Name*, Timothy Garton Ash describes Bahr and Kissinger as "the two Metternichs of détente"—in other words, as two arch-realists.[33] Thus Brandt's *Ostpolitik* can be thought of as the beginning of a centre-left realist current in West German foreign policy.

Like Adenauer's *Westbindung*, Brandt's *Ostpolitik* was a brilliant success. The Christian Democrats had initially been vehemently opposed to it and even created a private intelligence service to spy on Brandt.[34] But West German voters overwhelmingly endorsed *Ostpolitik* in the 1972 election—one of the few times foreign policy was to play a key role in a general election in the Federal Republic. In May 1974, Brandt was forced to resign after it emerged that one of his leading aides, Günter Guillaume, was an East German agent. He was replaced as chancellor by Helmut Schmidt, who had been finance minister in Brandt's government. But détente continued as the US and the Soviet Union signed the Strategic Arms Limitations Talks (SALT) treaties, which limited the numbers of long-range nuclear weapons, and negotiated a reduction in conventional forces stationed in Europe and a series of agreements on security, economic co-operation and humanitarian issues that culminated in the Helsinki Final Act of 1975.

In the US, the consensus around détente prompted a backlash from some Democrats who felt that American foreign policy had become too realist and was neglecting the promotion of democracy and human rights. Second-generation neoconservatives such as Scoop Jackson and the Coalition for a Democratic Majority attacked a version of US foreign policy that sought to downplay the ideological competition between the US and the Soviet Union.[35] Whereas Kissinger rejected what he saw as ideological crusades as a disruptive factor in international relations, these neoconservatives thought that détente was a betrayal of American values. Thus the backlash against détente produced a new idealist impetus in US foreign policy that would influence the Reagan administration in the 1980s.

In some ways, the West German version of détente was even more realist than the US version. In particular, in what has become known as the second phase of *Ostpolitik* under Schmidt, the transformative element of Bahr's strategy was largely forgotten as stability became an end in itself.[36] Gordon Craig writes that in the Helsinki negotiations the West Germans "took a more active interest than their Western allies in the economic, technological and environmental cooperation mapped out in the treaty but took virtually no interest in the human rights issues".[37] In fact, some German Social Democrats were so invested in *Ostpolitik* that they saw the emergence of Solidarity in Poland as a "threat to peace in Europe".[38] When General Wojciech Jaruzelski declared martial law in 1981, Bahr wrote that peace was more important than Poland.[39]

However, unlike in the US, there was little to no backlash against détente in West Germany. Rather, in the space created by détente, West

Germany under Schmidt began to pursue a more economically-driven foreign policy. Schmidt's success in stabilising the economy after the oil shock of 1973 had made it something of a model for other Western countries, and in the election campaign in 1976 he even used the slogan "Modell Deutschland". As West Germany's relative economic power increased, the Federal Republic also began to take greater initiative in foreign policy—in particular by seeking to increase co-ordination of economic policy, for example in creating the summit of leading developed economies that became the G7. It also signed a series of bilateral agreements with the GDR—which had become increasingly financially dependent on West Germany—that increased trade and eased travel between the two countries.

However, as the Cold War heated up at the end of the 1970s, West Germany was forced to change tack. In 1977, the Soviet Union had begun to replace its medium-range nuclear weapons with new SS-20 missiles that directly threatened western Europe and in particular West Germany. Although the SALT agreements had reduced the danger of an all-out nuclear war between the two superpowers, they had not included medium-range missiles or other so-called "theatre weapons" that threatened western Europe, while the Soviet Union continued to have overwhelming superiority in terms of conventional forces. To some West Germans like Schmidt, it seemed increasingly difficult to believe that the US would use nuclear weapons as a response to a conventional Soviet attack on the Federal Republic. In other words, in West Germany's case, the nuclear deterrent seemed less and less credible, leaving it more vulnerable than ever before in the Cold War.

In a speech at the International Institute for Strategic Studies in London in October 1977, Schmidt argued that NATO needed to rearm in Western Europe if the Warsaw Pact countries refused to disarm. Over the next two years, Schmidt helped bring about a shift in NATO strategy towards the Soviet Union to meet the new threat, and convinced the Americans to station new medium-range missiles of their own in Western Europe. In December 1979, NATO agreed to install Cruise and Pershing II missiles in various countries in Europe, including West Germany, if the Soviet SS-20s were not withdrawn by 1983. Though it had been prompted by the West German chancellor, there was huge opposition in West Germany to this so-called *Doppelbeschluß*, or "twin-track decision" and a massive campaign against the missile deployment began.

The peace movement—which two political scientists have called the "largest, most heterogeneous mass movement in the history of the Federal Republic"—illustrated how much the concept of "peace" resonated in West Germany.[40] The campaign reached its climax after Helmut Kohl had taken over as chancellor following the collapse of the Schmidt government in 1982. In October 1983, as the decision by the Bundestag about the missile deployment approached, 400,000 protesters, including Willy Brandt and the writer Günter Grass, took part in the largest ever demonstration in the history of the Federal Republic. Feelings were particularly strong in Schmidt's own party. At a party conference in November 1983, the Social Democrats voted by 583 votes to fourteen against the missile deployment—a rejection of Schmidt's policy and a partial reversal of the Bad Godesberg conference of 1959, at which the party had accepted rearmament and the *Westbindung*.

Schmidt's foreign policy illustrated the dilemmas West Germany faced during the Cold War. During the period of détente, the Federal Republic had begun to pursue a more economically-driven foreign policy and increasingly acted as a "trading state" that sought above all to maximise its own prosperity.[41] But it remained dependent on the US for its security. Once the strategic situation changed, therefore, West German foreign policy also had to change as strategic concerns overrode the economically-driven approach that Brandt and Schmidt had developed in the context of détente. Thus although West Germany had succeeded in increasing its freedom of manoeuvre—a key foreign-policy objective from Adenauer to Schmidt—the Cold War meant it still operated within hard constraints.

If the strategic environment was a hard constraint on West German foreign policy in the 1980s, the Nazi past was a soft constraint. In the 1960s and 1970s, West Germany had belatedly begun to debate the Nazi past. In particular, beginning in 1963 with the trial in Frankfurt of seventeen former guards at Auschwitz, the Federal Republic began to confront its responsibility for the Holocaust. But the story was one of escapism as well as engagement: even those who thought of themselves as challenging the silence of the 1950s about the Third Reich, such as the students who demonstrated on the streets of West Germany in the 1960s and 1970s, relativised the Nazi past in some ways.[42] Nevertheless, it was through the learning process prompted by the discussion of the

Nazi past that began in the 1960s that the Holocaust emerged as a powerful collective memory, as it did elsewhere in the West.[43]

One expression of this was the way that, from the 1970s onwards, West German heads of government and heads of state began to make gestures of contrition on behalf of the nation. When in December 1970, Brandt had kneeled down at the memorial to the Warsaw ghetto uprising in 1944, it was, as Jeffrey Herf puts it, "the first time that a West German chancellor had so publicly acknowledged and expressed remorse and atonement for what the Germans had done to the peoples of Eastern Europe and the Soviet Union during World War II."[44] In 1977, Helmut Schmidt became the first West German chancellor to deliver a speech at Auschwitz.[45] In a speech in May 1985, on the fortieth anniversary of the German surrender in World War II, President Richard von Weizsäcker, a Christian Democrat, gave what was to become the definitive statement of contrition about the Nazi past. Thus the Holocaust was entrenched in the "national memory of the German political establishment".[46]

However, as soon as the Holocaust seemed to have moved to the centre of West Germany's national identity, there was a backlash against it from the right. The summer after Weizsäcker's speech, Ernst Nolte, a West Berlin historian, argued in an essay published in the *Frankfurter Allgemeine Zeitung* that Nazi atrocities, and in particular the Holocaust, could only be understood in the context of other crimes in the twentieth century, in particular Stalinist terror. Nolte had previously written a book, *Fascism in its Epoch*, which argued that fascism was a European rather than specifically German phenomenon. He now argued that the Final Solution was in fact a defensive response to the Soviet Union's "class murder", which was its "logical and factual precursor".[47] Directly contradicting Weizsäcker, who had called for an ongoing process of remembering, Nolte said the Nazi past, like any other, should be allowed to "pass away".[48]

The essay led to a debate, subsequently known as the *Historikerstreit*, or "historians' debate", that was played out in the *feuilletons* of West Germany's leading newspapers for months. Although originally a historiographical debate about the "uniqueness" of the Holocaust, it came to focus on the question of whether it was time to draw a *Schlußstrich*, or final line, under Germany's Nazi past. Among Nolte's critics was the philosopher Jürgen Habermas, who accused Nolte and other conservative historians such as Michael Stürmer (a speechwriter for Helmut Kohl) of trying to "relativise" the Final Solution as part of a new revisionist nationalist agenda based on a "normalised" German history.[49] The *Historikerstreit* was largely an argument between left and right: the right wanted to "relativise"—or "historicise"—the Nazi past and "normalise" German national identity; the left insisted on the uniqueness of the Holocaust and the necessity of remembering.

The debate also had implications for West German foreign policy. By the 1980s, a consensus had emerged among the West German foreign policy establishment, based largely on Adenauer's approach to the rehabilitation of West Germany, about the foreign policy lessons of the Nazi past: a "culture of restraint" and in particular a rejection of the use of military force; the *Westbindung* and European integration; and responsibility for the security of Israel. But some had also sought to break out of the constraints of the Nazi past. For example, angered by the reaction to a planned deal to sell Leopard 2 main battle tanks to Saudi Arabia in 1981, Helmut Schmidt declared in private that West German foreign policy should no longer be "held hostage" to Auschwitz, though he was ultimately forced to abandon the deal.[50]

Partly in reaction to such attempts to break out of the soft constraint of the Nazi past, some on the left such as Joschka Fischer—a former member of the West German student movement—began to urge West Germany to make the Holocaust even more central to West German foreign policy. In an article in *Die Zeit* written at the same time as Weizsäcker's speech in May 1985 Fischer echoed Weizsäcker's description of 1945 as "liberation" and urged West Germans to develop a "democratic identity" by "consciously remembering" the Nazi past. "Only German responsibility for Auschwitz can be the essence of West German *raison d'état,*" he wrote. "Everything else comes afterwards."[51] Thus at the end of the Bonn Republic there emerged an embryonic centre-left idealist current in German foreign policy. But it was only later, in the so-called Berlin Republic created by reunification, that it would have an impact.

3

CONTINUITY AND CHANGE

Reunification in 1990 reopened the German question. For forty years, Germany had been divided, with the fault line of the Cold War running right through it. On a continent dominated by two external superpowers, both Germanies were vulnerable. As we have seen, the Federal Republic was a semi-sovereign state that was dependent on the US for its security. Thus security considerations alone required the Federal Republic to be part of the West. But the fall of the Berlin Wall and the transformation of Europe that ensued changed the parameters of German foreign policy. In fact, with the end of the Europe that had been created by the Big Three in Yalta in 1945, the geopolitical realities had changed as dramatically as they had with German unification in 1871.

With the inclusion of the former GDR, the Federal Republic had added 17 million people and had suddenly become significantly bigger than France or the UK. It was back to what Kurt-Georg Kiesinger, the West German chancellor from 1966 to 1969, had called its "kritische Größenordnung", or "critical size".[1] Moreover, the wider transformation of Europe also meant that Germany suddenly found itself relocated from *Grenzlage* back to *Mittellage*. As Stanley Hoffmann wrote in 1992 in a prescient analysis that echoed Disraeli's statement about the "German revolution" in 1871, "a unified Germany, even if its energies and resources were going to be temporarily absorbed by the rehabilitation of the former GDR, broke by its very existence the 'balance of imbalances' that had existed among the big three (or four) of western Europe. The reunification of the continent put Germany, not France, at the center."[2]

The idea of Germany as what historian Hans-Peter Schwarz called Europe's *Zentralmacht*, or "central power", evoked old fears.[3] In the background was the spectre of what had happened in Europe after 1871. Realist international relations theorists argued that, with the end of the Cold War, bipolarity would be replaced by multipolarity, which would in turn create instability and perhaps even an end to Europe's "long peace".[4] However, as liberal international relations theorists pointed out, the environment of 1990 was quite different to that of 1871. Even if Germany had returned to the *Mittellage*, it was now a "multilateral *Mittellage*".[5] Germany was now embedded in a network of institutions—in particular, the EU—that moderated state behaviour and produced stability. But might these institutions, which had been designed to contain a smaller Germany during the Cold War, now be overwhelmed?

Even before it happened, the prospect of German reunification was creating anxiety elsewhere in Europe. British Prime Minister Margaret Thatcher had welcomed the democratic revolution in East Germany but was alarmed by the possibility of a reunified Germany that suddenly became real in the weeks immediately following the fall of the Berlin Wall in November 1989. She believed Germany's "national character", as well as its size and position in the centre of Europe, made it an inherently "destabilising rather than a stabilising force in Europe".[6] She also worried, with some justification, that rapid reunification might undermine the position of Mikhail Gorbachev in the Soviet Union. However, with President George H. W. Bush in favour of German reunification and Gorbachev unable to stop it, she became almost completely isolated over the next few months.

Thatcher, who kept in her handbag a map showing Germany's 1937 borders and frequently took it out in meetings to illustrate what she called the "German problem", initially saw in French President François Mitterrand a possible ally who might help her stop—or at least slow down—German reunification. Mitterrand did share some of Thatcher's fears about Germany. According to the record by Thatcher's private secretary Charles Powell of a meeting at the Élysée Palace on 20 January 1990, Mitterrand told Thatcher that he "shared her analysis" of the situation and said he feared that Germany might attempt to regain territory it had lost as a result of the war and "might make even more ground than had Hitler".[7] However, in the months following the fall of the Berlin

Wall, Mitterrand came to see further European integration as a possible solution to the "German question".

Mitterrand's thinking was a continuation of that of French post-war leaders who had sought to constrain Germany through European integration. The EU was created in part to limit German power—in fact this may have initially been "the single most important driving force behind European integration".[8] In particular, by pooling its coal and steel production, Schuman had successfully rendered war between France and Germany "materially impossible". But after reunification, France had two contradictory fears: on the one hand that Germany might "go it alone", abandoning its European vocation and reverting to a Bismarckian foreign policy; and on the other hand that the reunified Germany might be too big for the institutions designed to contain it.[9]

Mitterrand concluded that deepening European integration would be the best way to cope with a united Germany. In particular, he thought that a single European currency was the only way for other European countries to regain the sovereignty they had already lost to Germany—and in particular to the Bundesbank. In fact, even before the fall of the Berlin Wall, he believed in the idea of monetary union. In September 1989, he had told Thatcher: "Without a common currency we are all of us—you and we—already subordinate to the Germans' will."[10] Thatcher, in contrast, thought that further integration would exacerbate rather than solve the problem of German power. She would later write in her memoirs that Germany was "more rather than less likely to dominate" in a federal Europe.[11] Thus the debate about how to respond to German reunification centred on the idea of European Monetary Union (EMU).

The idea had been around since the 1970s but had never become a reality. In particular, a committee led by Pierre Werner in 1970 had recommended a three-stage plan to create EMU within a decade through fixing exchange rates and coordinating monetary policy.[12] But the member states of what was then the European Economic Community (EEC), in particular France, had baulked at the idea of denationalising their currencies and, in doing so, giving up control of currency valuation—an important tool of economic statecraft. In addition, there were different views about how to design a single currency and especially what role a European central bank should play. In particular, West Germans were highly sceptical of the French model of a politically controlled and therefore inflation-prone central bank, and insisted on their own model of the independent, inflation-averse Bundesbank.

In a report published in April 1989, European Commission President Jacques Delors had made a new effort to map out a path to a single European currency and had recommended an intergovernmental conference to implement it, but left the timetable open. But the fall of the Berlin Wall six months later dramatically increased the urgency of the situation. Mitterrand immediately called on Kohl to agree to start serious negotiations on EMU before the end of 1990. Otherwise, Mitterrand said, "we will return to the world of 1913"—in other words, the classical German question.[13] Confronted with Germany's past in this way, Kohl backed down. At the crucial Strasbourg summit in December 1989, he agreed to convene an intergovernmental conference on EMU by the end of 1990. This was, according to David Marsh, "the essential deal" in the negotiation that produced the euro.[14]

The big unknown in the context of these dramatic changes in Europe, and given the long history of German question, was how resilient the Federal Republic's political culture was. In the forty years of its existence, West Germany had appeared to have made a decisive break with its past. In the context of the Cold War, it had committed to the West and developed a liberal democratic political culture. In other words, not only was the environment different in 1990 than in 1871, Germany itself was different. Kohl said it was "utter nonsense" to suggest that West Germany would become a "different republic" after reunification. But others were more sceptical and feared a resurgence of elements of what Theodor Adorno had called "the anti-civilisational, anti-Western undercurrent of the German tradition".[15]

In particular, many feared that the Federal Republic's attitude to the Nazi past would change after reunification. Thus, after the fall of the Berlin Wall, a debate began about the "normality" of the Berlin Republic. As in the *Historikerstreit* in the mid-1980s, the concept of "normality"—associated with the idea of a *Schlußstrich*—tended to be used by the right, while the left rejected it. Even those on the left who accepted that unification would inevitably produce a stronger sense of German national identity nevertheless rejected the concept of "normality". For example, the historian Christian Meier suggested that unification meant the end of West Germany's "post-national *Sonderweg*" and thus implied that the Bonn Republic was "abnormal". But he said the ongoing "burden of historical consciousness" excluded the possibility of "normality". "We are not a normal nation," he concluded.[16]

One of the most influential critics of the concept of "normality", going back to the *Historikerstreit*, was Jürgen Habermas—a former student of Adorno's. He had long advocated a "post-national" national identity based on Dolf Sternberger's idea of *Verfassungspatriotismus*, or constitutional patriotism. Habermas saw the memory of the Holocaust as crucial, because despite the progress that had been made in developing a democratic political culture in the Federal Republic, it was necessary to remember that "in Germany it was only after Auschwitz—and in a sense only because of the shock of this moral catastrophe—that democracy only began to take root."[17] The use of the concept of "normality" implicitly undermined this progress. In the old Federal Republic, he wrote, there had been an understanding of what he called the "dialectic of normalization": it was only the avoidance of a sense of "normality" that allowed "normality" to emerge.[18]

Habermas saw the democratic revolution in the GDR in 1989 as a "catching-up revolution"—in other words, one in which East Germans were simply attaining what their western counterparts long ago had achieved.[19] As unification became likely, he argued for a referendum based on Article 146 of the West German Basic Law, which would have created a new constitution for a united Germany. Instead, however, the six states of the GDR were simply "annexed" under Article 23 of the Basic Law. Habermas said that one of consequences of this lack of a "republican refounding" in 1990 was that "essential questions of political self-understanding—in particular the question of how we should understand the 'normality' of the approaching Berlin Republic—have remained open."[20]

Habermas argued that some on the right had, as a result, used this "normative deficit" as an opportunity to resume the argument for "normalisation" that they had made during the *Historikerstreit*. In 1991 he wrote that they now saw "a chance to reverse the change in mentality that has taken place in the last few decades and to put the enlarged Germany on a course towards a 'normalization' that will finally free us from the trauma of the mass crimes we committed and restore our national innocence."[21] He suggested that those on the right who argued for "normality" were revisionists who wanted to turn the period between 1945 and 1989 into an aberration that embodied "the forced abnormality of a defeated and divided nation".[22] In short, they saw the Bonn Republic as kind of *Sonderweg*.[23]

The idea of a *Schlußstrich* was assumed to imply a foreign policy that would be "normal" in the sense that it was more confident, or less inhibited by the Nazi past, than that of the Bonn Republic. At the symbolic level, this could mean a reduction in the expressions of contrition such as those made by Brandt and Weizsäcker. But, in more substantial policy terms, the left also feared that "normality" could mean two other things. First, it could mean a loosening of the *Westbindung* that had begun in the 1950s under Adenauer with the Federal Republic's membership in NATO and European integration. Second, it could mean a resurgence of German militarism, which some assumed went hand-in-hand with German nationalism. Thus those on the left who opposed the idea of "normality" were making a plea for continuity in German foreign policy.

During the Kohl era, the first of these two foreign-policy fears—a loosening of the *Westbindung*—did not materialise. Germany remained firmly part of the West. Indeed, together with President Mitterrand, Kohl continued to press ahead with European integration and following reunification agreed to take perhaps the most momentous step yet in the history of European integration: the creation of the euro. It is sometimes said that there was a quid pro quo: the euro for reunification. In reality, it was not that simple. Nevertheless, the single currency was created in the context of reunification and would probably not have happened without it—or at least nowhere near as soon. In particular, it is unlikely that France and Germany would have overcome their differences about how to design a single currency.

The Bundesbank's view was that a single currency should be the final step in a long process of economic co-ordination and convergence that would culminate in political union—the so-called *Krönungstheorie*, or "crowning theory". France, on the other hand, wanted to retain sovereignty in a *Europe des patries*. If it had not needed French support for reunification, Germany is unlikely to have agreed to brush aside the revered Bundesbank's fears and move ahead so fast with EMU and in particular with the intergovernmental conference that Kohl and Mitterrand agreed at the Strasbourg summit in December 1989. "If unification had not happened, it is highly unlikely that France would have been able to persuade Kohl to agree the EMU timetable to replace the D-Mark by the euro," writes David Marsh.[24]

However, although Germany agreed to create a single currency rather sooner than it would have liked, and before a political union had been created, it was able to get its way in other respects—so much so that the

German finance minister Theo Waigel told Germans in 1991 that "we are bringing the D-Mark into Europe."[25] The new European central bank would be modelled on the Bundesbank—that is, it would be independent of political control and would be mandated to maintain price stability above all else—and, as if to symbolise this, would be based in Frankfurt. "Our stability policy has become the leitmotif for the future European monetary order," Waigel said.[26] Germany also insisted on what became the so-called convergence criteria, which among other things limited government budget deficits to 3 per cent of GDP and the ratio of government debt-to-GDP to 60 per cent. It also insisted on a "no bailout" clause, which specified that member states should not be liable for, nor assume, the commitments or debts of any other.

Thus the embryonic single European currency that emerged from the intergovernmental conference at the end of 1991 was based on a compromise between French and German views. It was, as Stanley Hoffmann put it, a "compromise between the French insistence on a full and genuine monetary union, with a central bank and a single currency, and German insistence on a prior rapprochement of economic policies, on an independent bank, and on some institutional reform".[27] The compromise between France and Germany was codified in the Maastricht Treaty of 1992, which laid the foundation for the EMU and with it the replacement of the deutsche mark by the euro by 1999.

In March 1990, as Germany moved rapidly towards reunification, Jürgen Habermas had written a famous article about what he called "DM nationalism".[28] He worried that a new form of "chubby-faced" economic nationalism could usurp the fragile post-national national identity based on the concept of "constitutional patriotism" that had gradually emerged in the Federal Republic since 1949. Habermas argued that the other elements on which post-war West German national identity was based—for example anti-communism—had weakened since the end of the 1960s. That left only the Federal Republic's economic achievements since the *Wirtschaftswunder*, or economic miracle—symbolised by the deutsche mark—as a popular source of national pride.

However, just as this economic nationalism had emerged, Germany agreed to abandon the deutsche mark for a euro that they were promised would be just as hard. Far from slowing down European integration, therefore, reunification had accelerated it. Some, especially outside Europe, were sceptical about the single currency. In what Mary Elise

Sarotte calls the "mad rush" to agree the terms of monetary union, European leaders such as Kohl and Mitterrand, who had little understanding of economics, created a single currency that had neither the ability to respond to crises nor real political coordination.[29] The economist Martin Feldstein even argued that it would create conflict within Europe and between Europe and the US.[30] But for the moment, Kohl seemed to have been proven right that there was a symbiotic relationship between Germany and Europe.

If Germany's *Europapolitik* in the 1990s was characterised by continuity, however, its foreign policy was nevertheless undergoing change in other respects. In particular, Germany came under increasing pressure from its NATO allies, especially the United States, to take greater responsibility for solving global problems. Above all, as ethnic and regional conflicts flared up in the 1990s, above all in the Balkans, Germany came under pressure to modify its attitude towards the use of military force. As a result, in the mid-1990s the debate about "normality" focused increasingly on the second of the left's foreign-policy fears: what Habermas called the "creeping militarisation" of German foreign policy.[31]

In the context of the Cold War, West Germany had been able to avoid the difficult questions that were now being raised about "responsibility". Article 26 of the Basic Law prohibited the Federal Republic from fighting wars of aggression; Article 87a, added after West Germany joined NATO in 1955, restricted Germany's armed forces to a defensive role. It meant Germany could use its military only if it or another NATO country was directly attacked. During the Cold War, West Germany had been relatively happy with this role, and so had its allies. But following reunification, expectations began to change. While some in Europe worried about the power of the new, reunified Germany, others, particularly in the United States, wanted it to play a more active role beyond Europe and to become, as President Bush put it, a "partner in leadership".

A tension therefore emerged between Germany's reluctance to use military force and its commitment to multilateralism, and in particular Atlanticism. This tension, which would define the foreign policy-debates of the 1990s in Germany, first came to the surface during the Gulf War in 1991, which the German public overwhelmingly opposed. By referring to Article 87a—which stipulated that Germany could not participate in "out of area" operations—Chancellor Kohl was able to hold off American pressure for German military involvement. For the moment, Germany reverted to its Cold War role: it would foot the bill while other countries did the fighting. However, Washington made it clear that next time a cheque would not be enough. In the years following that war, Germany came under increasing pressure to take a more active role in solving ethnic and regional conflicts.

Over the next decade, Germany took a series of baby steps towards a more interventionist foreign policy. The first were in Cambodia in 1992 and Somalia in 1993, where Germany sent troops as part of unarmed UN humanitarian operations. It was above all in the Balkans, however, that the shift to a more interventionist approach played out. As Yugoslavia began to disintegrate from 1991 onwards—helped along, some argue, by Germany's unilateral recognition of an independent Croatia in 1991—ethnic conflicts between the Serbs, Croats and Muslims, particularly in Bosnia, re-emerged. In 1992, as President Slobodan Milosevic began to try to create a geographically contiguous and ethnically pure Greater Serbia, the United Nations dispatched a peacekeeping force to the region.

Against this background, the concept of "normality" was increasingly associated by the right with the idea of *Bündnisfähigkeit*—a term denoting the ability to fulfil commitments as a member of NATO. One of the first to use the concept of "normality" in this way was Karl Lamers, who, as foreign-policy spokesman of the Christian Democrat parliamentary group, in August 1990 argued that Germany should "accept that the military power plays a role even in today's world" and "become a normal member of the international community".[32] Similarly, following the Gulf War in 1991, Karl-Heinz Hornhues, the deputy chairman of the Christian Democrat parliamentary group, proposed a constitutional amendment to allow German troops to participate in peacekeeping operations. This, he said, would enable the Federal Republic to become "a normal member of the alliance" and "completely capable of fulfilling its commitments as a member of the alliance".[33]

Helmut Kohl's approach was, essentially, to push Germany to take greater responsibility on the global stage but to try to remain within the Federal Republic's traditional foreign-policy "culture of restraint". That meant, firstly, that any military deployment should be within a multilateral framework and, above all, be subject to the approval of the United Nations. Secondly, it meant that Germany should deploy its military with extreme caution and in particular take into account sensitivities about German history. This approach coalesced into the so-called Kohl doctrine, according to which German troops could serve "out of area", but not in any territory occupied by the Wehrmacht in World War II. Of course, the former Yugoslavia was precisely such a territory.

As the situation in the Balkans worsened and Germany came under increasing pressure to play its part in peacekeeping operations, the Kohl government was itself forced to go beyond the Kohl doctrine, beginning in mid-1992 with the enforcement of UN sanctions against Yugoslavia. Initially, German crews were used to man Airborne Warning and Control Systems (AWACS) reconnaissance aircraft monitoring and later enforcing the "no-fly" zone in Bosnia. In 1994, NATO asked Germany to use its Tornado jets in support of its operations and for German assistance in a non-combat role in the event of an evacuation of UNPROFOR, the United Nations' peacekeeping force in Bosnia. The same year, the Constitutional Court clarified the constitutional position, ruling that Germany's armed forces could participate in any "out of area" operations sanctioned by the UN, subject to Bundestag approval.

This incremental shift in German foreign policy—sometimes described as "modified continuity"—was driven largely by events and pressure from Germany's allies.[34] German politicians generally followed events rather than shaped them, often equivocating and passing the buck to the judiciary where possible. However, in so far as German politicians influenced events, it was the right that drove the change. More than anyone, it was the Christian Democrat defence minister Volker Rühe who made the case for the use of the German military to help resolve international conflicts and for the transformation of the Bundeswehr for that role. In doing so, he even referred to the Holocaust: just as the victims of Nazi concentration camps had been liberated only by the Allies, he argued, so foreign intervention was required to liberate the victims of concentration camps in Bosnia.

Meanwhile, fearing a "militarisation" of German foreign policy, the left opposed change. Although most of the leading figures in the Social Democrats had long reconciled themselves to German membership of NATO, they still resisted the idea of "out of area" operations or of the Bundeswehr becoming an "army of intervention". For example, in the debate in the Bundestag on the use of Tornados in June 1995, passed by 386 votes to 258, Rudolf Scharping, then the Social Democrat leader and later defence minister, argued that sending Tornados to the Balkans would be inappropriate because of Germany's history. Meanwhile, the Greens—the party that had emerged from the peace movement in the early 1980—were still in favour of dissolving NATO and abolishing the Bundeswehr as part of a "consistently pacifist" approach to foreign policy.[35]

In arguing against a shift towards greater use of military force, some on the left used the concept of "civilian power"—but in the process distorted it.[36] Maull had argued that the project of civilising international relations might sometimes demand the use of military force and that a "civilian power" should therefore have the ability and willingness to contribute to military interventions. But some left-wing opponents of a greater role for the Bundeswehr argued that involvement in "out of area" operations would violate the idea of "civilian power" and thus misunderstood the implications of the idea for the question of military force. In what Maull calls a "pacifist redefinition" of the concept of "civilian power", they used it to make a case for Germany as a *Friedensmacht*, or "force for peace".

However, in the mid-1990s, some on the left began to rethink their attitude to the use of military force and embrace the idea of humanitarian intervention. In particular, some members of the "realist" faction in the Green party drew different lessons from German history, and in particular from the Holocaust, than others on the left. The faction, which had formed in the early 1980s in opposition to what it called the "fundamentalists" and become increasingly influential within the Green party, also had a different attitude towards the West and in particular towards US power. Cohn-Bendit, the intellectual leader of the "realist" faction, said in 1993 that he was a "child of D-Day" who would not have existed without the US-led invasion of occupied France. Echoing Rühe's arguments, Cohn-Bendit said that, by opposing intervention in Bosnia, the Greens risked being "in the tradition of the appeasement that led to the destruction of the Jews".[37]

The key figure in this rethink, alongside Cohn-Bendit, was the Green leader Joschka Fischer—who until then had been one of the harshest critics of the Kohl government's foreign policy. The son of a butcher, Fischer had dropped out of school and took part in the student rebellion in West Germany in 1968. In the 1970s he was a revolutionary socialist who fought the police on the streets of Frankfurt, where he met, and became close to, Cohn-Bendit. After members of the West German New Left became involved in terrorism in the 1970s—and in particular after the anti-Semitic Entebbe hijacking in 1976, in which two West Germans he knew had been involved—Fischer withdrew from politics. But though he did not feel strongly about environmental issues, he saw the Green Party as a way to re-engage in politics and in 1983 he became a Green member of Bundestag.

When in 1985 Fischer wrote that "only German responsibility for Auschwitz can be the essence of West German *raison d'état*," he was seeking above all to prevent a "remilitarisation" of German foreign policy. Even in 1993 Cohn-Bendit's support for military intervention in Bosnia seemed "out of date" to him.[38] But after the massacre by the Serbs of 7,000 Bosnian Muslims at Srebrenica in 1995, the worst atrocity in Europe since World War II, he changed his mind.[39] Fischer would later say that, for a few days after news emerged of what had happened in Srebrenica, he had difficulties looking at himself in the mirror. "I was asking myself the same question that I had once asked my parents," he said.[40] The 6,000-word open letter he subsequently wrote, in which he urged his party colleagues to "resist" the "new fascism" in the Balkans and support military intervention, sparked an intense debate that would last for the next six months.

It was from the debate within the Greens about military intervention in Bosnia that a new centre-left idealist current in German foreign-policy thinking emerged. Fischer was as committed to the *Westbindung* and as passionate a pro-European as Kohl—thus Winkler would refer to a "posthumous Adenauerian left".[41] But, influenced by Habermas's thinking, Fischer also argued that Germany had a special responsibility to remember, and learn the lessons of, the Holocaust. Even as Fischer changed his attitude to the use of force, however, he continued to reject the concept of "normality" in favour of a kind of German exceptionalism or "negative nationalism" based on Germany's "Holocaust identity".[42] This centre-left idealist current would reach the high point of its influence on German foreign policy when Fischer became foreign minister in the "red-green" coalition.

When, after sixteen years in power, Helmut Kohl was finally voted out of office and the Social Democrat Gerhard Schröder became chancellor at the head of the first-ever "red-green" coalition in Germany in the autumn of 1998, Germany was in the middle of a yet another *Schlußstrich* debate. Towards the end of the 1990s, against the background of the debate about the planned Holocaust memorial in the centre of Berlin—the new capital of the reunified Germany—some once again began to challenge the role that the Nazi past played in German public life. In particular, in a speech in the Paulskirche in Frankfurt in October 1998, the writer Martin Walser had called the memorial a "football-field-sized nightmare" and rejected the "instrumentalisation of Auschwitz" for political purposes.[43]

Walser's views were identified with those of the new chancellor, who, unlike his predecessor or Fischer, seemed implicitly to endorse Walser's argument that the Holocaust was a private matter rather than the basis for policy. Schröder was of the same generation as Fischer—the so-called *Achtundsechziger*—and had first made a name for himself as an opponent of the deployment of US missiles to West Germany in the 1980s. But Schröder had a quite different attitude towards German history to Fischer. In his first speech as chancellor, he spoke of the "self-confidence of a grown-up nation" that would pursue its national interests, particularly within the EU.[44] As a result, he was often identified in the media with the idea of an "uninhibited nation"—that is, one that that would pursue a "normal" foreign policy.[45] Whereas Fischer emphasised continuity in German foreign policy, Schröder seemed to promise change.[46]

It was against this background that the "red-green" government faced its first foreign-policy crisis. By the autumn of 1998, the Serbian province of Kosovo had emerged as the new flashpoint in the Balkans. A humanitarian catastrophe loomed as ethnic Albanians—who made up 90 per cent of the province's population—fled their towns and villages to escape Serb soldiers and paramilitaries. By the time Kohl was voted out of office on 27 September, 300,000 Kosovar Albanians had been driven from their homes and preparations were being made for a NATO attack on Yugoslavia. Even before they had been sworn in, Schröder and Fischer reluctantly succumbed to pressure from the Clinton administration and agreed in principle to send German troops into combat in order to demonstrate to Milosevic that NATO was united.

The prospect of a military intervention against Milosevic split the left not just in Germany but throughout the West. Some accepted the argument that it was legitimate to undertake a military intervention, unilaterally if necessary, where crimes were being committed that, as Michael

Walzer put it, "shock the moral conscience of mankind".[47] A significant number of those on the left around Europe who most eloquently and loudly made this case for humanitarian intervention were veterans of the student movements of 1968 such as Daniel Cohn-Bendit and Bernard Kouchner, the founder of *Médecins Sans Frontières*, who would become the first permanent UN administrator in Kosovo after the war was over, and later the French foreign minister. Thus Paul Berman later called it the "68ers' war".[48]

For Germany, involvement in the NATO military intervention was particularly difficult. Firstly, although Germany had gradually reconciled itself to the idea of using its military abroad, it had until then only been used for peacekeeping purposes rather than war fighting. Secondly, the 1994 Constitutional Court decision had cleared the German military to participate in "out of area" operations, but only with UN approval. However, because of Russian opposition, a Security Council resolution authorising military action was unlikely. Some argued that the lack of a Security Council resolution made it, in legal terms, a war of aggression. However, from a broader perspective, a refusal to participate in military action would also have violated one of the most fundamental principles of German post-war foreign policy by causing a major rift within NATO.

It was Joschka Fischer who, more than any other member of the "red-green" government, made the case for the NATO military intervention and for German participation in it. Fischer's response to Kosovo, once again informed by the Nazi past, was a logical development of his stand on Srebrenica. He would certainly have preferred the backing of the UN Security Council, but it was also clear to him that if Germany had to intervene without UN approval in order to prevent genocide, it should. "If people are being massacred", he said in an interview in January 1999, "you cannot mutter about having no mandate."[49] During the war, as the tortuous debate within the Green party about war and peace continued, he declared, "I didn't just learn 'never again war.' I also learned, 'never again Auschwitz'."[50]

However, it was not just Fischer who drew parallels with the Nazi past. In fact, much of the debate about German participation in the military intervention was about the right lessons to learn from the Nazi past: "never again war" or "never again Auschwitz". Frank Schirrmacher, the editor of the *feuilleton* of the *Frankfurter Allgemeine Zeitung* would later write that "in Germany, unlike in other countries, people justify this war almost exclusively on the basis of Auschwitz."[51] While some such as Fischer justified their support for military intervention by reference to Auschwitz, others justified their opposition to it on the basis of a different reading of the lessons of the Nazi past. Thus the public argument about the Kosovo War became a hyper-moral one that made a debate about a crisis in a foreign country a somewhat narcissistic debate about German identity.

One person who did not invoke the Nazi past, however, was Schröder. "I thought it was wrong," he later said. "Auschwitz is something very unique and to make a comparison is to question the uniqueness of Auschwitz."[52] Instead, Schröder justified German involvement in the war using the language of "normality". For example, in a speech at the Munich Security Conference in February 1999—just before Operation Allied Force began—Schröder said Germany did not want to pursue a *Sonderweg* and was ready to take responsibility "as a normal ally".[53] Schröder's use of the language of "normality" showed that some on the left were now also prepared to apply it to German foreign policy as Christian Democrats had done from the early 1990s. Crucially, however, Schröder, like the right, equated "normality" with *Bündnisfähigkeit*.

After an agonised debate, particularly among the Greens, the Bundestag voted to approve German participation the operation. On 24 March 1999, after further diplomacy had failed and the situation on the ground had worsened, four German Tornados armed with anti-radar missiles attacked Serbian anti-aircraft defences. For the first time since 1945, Germany was at war. Although German crews would fly only 436 out of a total of 37,565 sorties during the war and only launch one-thousandth of the total missiles used during the conflict, Germany had certainly taken a difficult step.[54] But the agreement between Fischer and Schröder about policy masked the difference between two visions of German identity and foreign policy. The difference between them centred on the significance of the Holocaust in determining Germany's present and future role in the world.

A decade after reunification, German foreign policy was characterised by a mixture of continuity and change. The fears that some had had at the time of reunification had not been realised. In particular, the *Westbindung* had not loosened. Germany remained part of NATO, which had in the meantime enlarged to include the Czech Republic, Hungary and Poland.

Following reunification, European integration had also deepened. When the euro was launched on schedule on 1 January 1999, the French strategy seemed to have worked—Germany was now even more deeply embedded in European institutions than before reunification and had even abandoned the beloved deutsche mark. The German question, which had been reopened by the fall of the Wall, appeared to have been resolved—or at least was no longer acute.

There had been a dramatic change in Germany's attitude to the use of military force. The journalist Theo Sommer even wrote in *Die Zeit* that Kosovo had made Germany "a different republic".[55] But Germany seemed to be converging with its allies and in particular with France and the UK on the use of military force—and in that sense was becoming more "normal". In fact, in order to demonstrate its commitment to its allies, it had taken difficult steps such as the one to send troops into combat in Kosovo, which seemed to confirm what Heinrich August Winkler, writing in 2000, called a "European normalisation of Germany".[56] It also seemed to confirm the principle of "Never again Auschwitz" as the basis of German foreign policy. This was a centre-left idealist foreign policy based on a commitment to the *Westbindung* and the idea of atonement for Auschwitz as Germany's *raison d'état*.

Germany could also still claim to be a "civilian power". It remained committed to multilateralism and in particular to the EU and NATO. It had begun to use military force more readily than previously, but had done so within a multilateral framework and above all to prevent humanitarian catastrophes. This was not necessarily incompatible with a "civilian power" identity. In fact, it could be argued that during the Kosovo conflict, Germany had for the first time acted as an *Ordnungsmacht*—that is, a power that intervened to maintain the global order—and thus strengthened its claim to be a "civilian power". While some in Germany, particularly on the left, were uncomfortable with the new interventionism in German foreign policy, its NATO allies and European partners welcomed it. In short, although by the end of the 1990s, Germany seemed to be becoming a "different republic", it seemed more deeply integrated in the West than ever.

4

PERPETRATORS AND VICTIMS

Four years later, things looked very different. By the time the US invaded Iraq in the spring of 2003, relations between Germany and the US had been "poisoned", as US National Security Adviser Condoleezza Rice put it in September 2002.[1] Germany had not only opposed the US on a matter that the latter considered vital to its national security, but also formed a counter-coalition against it as part of what one international relations theorist called a strategy of "soft balancing".[2] With the Iraq war, writes Stephen Szabo, "the post-Cold War period in the German-US relationship ended".[3] Henry Kissinger wrote that he had never thought that the relationship could deteriorate so quickly and worried that "a kind of anti-Americanism may become a permanent temptation of German politics."[4] The rift between Germany and the US over Iraq even led some analysts to worry that it "could signal the end of 'the West' as a meaningful concept".[5]

A big part of the explanation of what had happened was that US foreign policy had changed after 2000. Even before 9/11, President George W. Bush had already alienated many Europeans by refusing to ratify the Kyoto Protocol and to sign up to the International Criminal Court. But the attacks created a "powerful wave of support for the United States" in Europe in general and in Germany in particular.[6] After September 11, Schröder promised the US Germany's "unlimited solidarity" and, after the first-ever invocation of Article 5 of the North Atlantic Treaty, NATO's collective security clause, Germany committed troops to what became the International Security Assistance Force (ISAF) mission in Afghanistan. Schröder put his own job on the line when he called a vote of confidence in conjunction with the vote on the Afghanistan deployment. *Bündnistreue*, or loyalty to the alliance, remained the guiding principle of German foreign policy.

However, over the next eighteen months an unprecedented rift between Germany and the US opened up, which exposed deeper, longer-term changes in the relationship that had been taking place in the decade between reunification and 9/11. The underlying reality was that Germany and the US were no longer as important to each other as they were during the Cold War. Regardless of who was in the White House in Washington or the chancellery in Berlin, Germany and the US simply needed each other less than they did before. This long-term shift was dramatically exacerbated as American and German threat perceptions and strategic culture diverged after 9/11. But this divergence was itself also in part a consequence of a shift in German identity that was taking place at the same time.

It was during the summer of 2002, though it remains unclear exactly when, that Gerhard Schröder decided to publicly oppose the Iraq War regardless of the circumstances under which it might take place. After nearly four years in office, Schröder looked set to lose the general election that was due to take place that autumn and opinion polls showed a vast majority of Germans were opposed to an invasion of Iraq.[7] Schröder later said that the pivotal factor in his decision was the way that the arguments used by the Bush administration to justify the invasion appeared to shift during the course of 2002. Initially, it had claimed a link existed between Iraq and al-Qaeda. However, that claim was subsequently dropped and the focus shifted to Saddam Hussein's alleged possession of weapons of mass destruction, which, however, could not yet be proven.[8]

Schröder launched his election campaign with a speech in Hanover in August 2002 that was unprecedented in the history of post-war German foreign policy. In it, he distanced himself from the United States and spoke of a "Deutscher Weg", or "German Way"—as opposed to the "American Way". "The era in which we look to America and others as a model for our economy is over," he said. Turning to Iraq, he declared that "I will not lead this country into adventures."[9] Never before in the history of the Federal Republic had a chancellor so publicly distanced himself from the US on such an important issue, or criticised the US in such a general way. It was also a break with the foreign policy of the "red-green" government up to that point, which had been distinguished by an emphasis on the importance of multilateralism and in particular of *Bündnistreue*. Schröder could not have made it plainer that the period of "unconditional solidarity" with the United States after 9/11 was now over.

In addition, by using the concept of the "German Way", Schröder was striking an unmistakably nationalist tone, although he would later deny that this was his intention. Looking back after he left office, he claimed that he had intended, firstly, to contrast the German social market economy with the Anglo-Saxon free market economic model, and, secondly, to refer to "Willy Brandt's peace policy".[10] He said that, in so far as he was talking about foreign policy, he was attempting to draw a contrast not so much with the United States as with the opposition Christian Democrats, who had been less openly critical of Bush. But by using the concept of a "German way", he was, whether consciously or unconsciously, invoking an idea of an alternative to Western ideas and models that had been a key motif of German nationalism going back to the nineteenth century.

It worked. The rhetoric of "peace" resonated with German voters and Schröder continued his campaign in the same vein. The focus on Iraq shifted attention away from Germany's economic difficulties, and in particular unemployment, which had reached 3.5 million by 2002. Crucially, it helped win much-needed support among the far left and among east Germans whom the Social Democrats had lost to the Christian Democrats and the Partei des Demokratischen Sozialismus (PDS), the former East German Communist Party.[11] Polls showed that East Germans were even more opposed to an invasion of Iraq, and even more anti-American, than West Germans. By the end of August, the SPD had caught up in the polls, and, in the election at the end of September, Schröder was narrowly re-elected—a remarkable achievement given how far he had been trailing in polls when the campaign began.

Just as Schröder criticised Joschka Fischer's reference to Auschwitz to justify the Kosovo War, Fischer later criticised Schröder's use of the concept of a "German way" to oppose the Iraq War.[12] Fischer was also opposed to the idea of an invasion of Iraq, but was disturbed by the chancellor's use of nationalist and anti-American rhetoric and did not want the German "no" to the war to turn into a "no" to NATO. He was also worried about Berlin becoming isolated—at this point not even French President Jacques Chirac had committed himself one way or the other. Thus Fischer attempted to develop a more nuanced position. In an interview with the *Spiegel* at the end of 2002, he floated the idea of agreeing in the United Nations Security Council to military action against Iraq, while refusing to commit German troops. However, Schröder ruled out this option.

At the beginning of November, after eight weeks of negotiations, the UN Security Council unanimously passed Resolution 1441, which reiterated that Iraq would face "serious consequences" if it did not comply with its disarmament obligations under previous resolutions, and sent UN weapons inspectors back to Iraq. In January 2003, Germany took up a non-veto-bearing seat on the UN Security Council and, the following month, the rotating chairmanship of the Security Council. But at an appearance in the north German town of Goslar in the run-up to another election, this time in the state of Lower Saxony, Schröder stated publicly that Germany would vote against military action in the Security Council—an even stronger statement than he had made up to that point. Fortunately for him, France and Russia joined Germany in opposing a resolution authorising military force in February—and thus rescued Germany from isolation.

In fact, despite Schröder's loud opposition to the war, Germany did quietly provide the United States with significant military assistance. Germany agreed to send German AWACS reconnaissance aircraft to patrol the skies over Turkey; after initial opposition, provided missiles for Patriot missile batteries that were also sent to Turkey in case it was attacked by Iraq; and used its navy to protect waterways for American ships en route to the Persian Gulf. More controversially, it would later emerge that two German intelligence agents had remained in Baghdad during the war and secretly provided information they gathered—including details of Iraqi military units and weapons located in the city—to the US military. The information was passed through another German intelligence officer, who was stationed in the headquarters of General Tommy Franks, the American commander of the invasion, in Qatar.[13]

Many outside Germany welcomed Schröder's opposition to the Iraq War. But the debate about the merits of the war obscured the significance of the break in German foreign policy that had taken place in the run-up to it. Just as in the debate about the use of military force in the 1990s, when some on the German left had reduced the idea of "civilian power" to that of a *Friedensmacht*, or "force for peace", many, both in Germany and beyond it, now welcomed Germany's opposition to the use of military force in Iraq as consistent with the traditional values of German foreign policy. But the reality was more complicated. In fact, Germany's opposition to the Iraq War—especially the way Schröder expressed it—represented a profound break with German foreign policy up to that point. In a sense, Germany's approach to the Iraq crisis actually undermined its claim to be a "civilian power".

At first glance, it seemed as if Germany had chosen Europe—and in particular France—over the US. In the past, Germany had carefully positioned itself between France and the US in order to avoid choosing between the two—a balancing act that had become harder since the end of the Cold War, particularly since 9/11. But in 2003, Germany had for the first time openly aligned itself with France against the US. Szabo writes that "Europe had taken priority over Germany's transatlantic tie with the United States."[14] Schröder himself later spoke of his sense of a "European mission".[15] But Germany had not exactly followed France—if anything, it had led it. Schröder was already publicly opposed to the US invasion of Iraq in the summer of 2002—that is, before President Chirac had made up his mind.

Moreover, Europe was itself split down the middle rather than united behind France and Germany. At the end of January 2003, US Defense Secretary Donald Rumsfeld famously referred to an "old Europe" that opposed the US and a "new Europe" that supported it. A week later the heads of government of eight EU member states, including Spanish Prime Minister José Maria Aznar and British Prime Minister Tony Blair, signed a letter of support for US policy that was published in the *Wall Street Journal*. The "letter of eight" was followed by another letter of support from the "Vilnius 10"—a group of ten Baltic, central European and Balkan states. In short, if France and Germany were attempting to lead Europe in opposition to US policy, it was a disastrous failure.

This failure reflected an internal shift within the EU that had taken place in the previous decade. Part of the reason Franco-German leadership had functioned in the past was because of what Stanley Hoffmann had called the "balance of imbalances". Moreover, because France and West Germany took opposite positions on many issues, it meant that, if they could agree, they could also co-opt other member states. But with the end of the Cold War and EU enlargement, it had become harder for France and Germany "to cover the full spectrum of major divergences", as François Heisbourg puts it.[16] In the 1990s, EU member states had also adapted to the absence of Franco-German leadership and found new ways of working. Thus when Chirac and Schröder tried to revive Franco-German leadership in the context of Iraq, it was rejected by other member states.

Thus what had happened during the Iraq crisis was not quite as simple as Germany having sided with Europe against the US. Clearly, the Bush administration had broken with US foreign-policy tradition and pursued a more unilateral approach than its predecessors, in particular the Clinton administration. But Germany had also sacrificed multilateralism in order to oppose the Iraq War—the opposite of what it had done on Kosovo. Schröder's opposition to the Iraq War was, as Szabo puts it, "a striking break with the tradition of multilateralism in German policy".[17] In fact, there was a paradoxical symmetry between Germany and the US: while Bush and Schröder had opposing views on the substance, they were both prepared to act without reference to multilateral institutions such as the United Nations Security Council.

One way to think of the shift that had taken place in German foreign policy is in terms of its preferences and what might be called its meta-level preferences. Since reunification, German preferences such as reluctance to use military force had been increasingly difficult to reconcile with meta-level preferences such as multilateralism, which had framed the foreign policy of the Federal Republic since its creation in 1949 and had led analysts such as Hanns Maull to describe it as a "civilian power". In the 1990s, Germany had tended to make compromises on its preferences (such as its reluctance to use military force) in order to stick to its meta-level preferences (such as multilateralism). The significance of the Iraq War was that, for the first time, Germany compromised on its meta-level preferences. Part of the reason for this was a subtle shift in German national identity that was taking place around the time of the Iraq War.

Throughout the history of the Federal Republic, collective memories in which Germans appear as perpetrators had competed with collective memories in which Germans appear as victims. Chronologies of these competing collective memories usually divide the history of the Federal

Republic into three phases: the early post-war period (essentially the 1950s), which was dominated by collective memories of German victimhood; a second period from the 1960s onwards, during which, prompted by events such as the Auschwitz trials, collective memories in which Germans were perpetrators became dominant; and finally a third phase, beginning around the millennium, in which collective memories of German victimhood re-emerged.[18]

Eric Langenbacher has identified 1999 as the "critical juncture" at which the dominant collective theme of Germans as perpetrators gave way to the theme of Germans as victims. According to his periodisation of collective memory in the Federal Republic, there have been two phases, "divided loosely around the 1999 return of the capital to Berlin".[19] He argues that the first decade after German reunification in 1990 was characterised by the "continuation, culmination and institutionalization of Holocaust memory" that had begun in the 1960s and achieved "cultural hegemony" in the 1980s.[20] This "Holocaust identity" seems in retrospect to have reached its high point in the debate about the Kosovo War in 1999. But after 2002, Holocaust memory decreased in significance while the memory of German suffering increased in significance.

Whereas the debate about Kosovo was dominated by collective memories in which Germans appeared as perpetrators, the debate about Iraq in the second half of 2002 and the first half of 2003 was dominated by collective memories in which Germans appeared as victims. During this period there was what one American newspaper reporter called "an outpouring of memory" that had the effect of "changing the public view of World War II" and "strengthening the German opposition against a threatened war in Iraq".[21] This outpouring of memory centred not on the Holocaust, as in the case of Kosovo, but on German suffering during World War II, particularly as a result of the Allied bombing of German cities. The reporter wrote: "For the first time, many Germans are openly considering themselves not just as perpetrators of wars, but as victims of war."[22]

The catalyst for this public discussion of German victimhood was the publication in November 2002 of the historian Jörg Friedrich's book *Der Brand*.[23] The book, which was serialised in *Bild*, Germany's bestselling tabloid newspaper, and quickly became a bestseller, described the Allied bombing campaign in a way that was not just vivid and emotive but also, more problematically, used language that evoked the Nazis and in particular the Holocaust. For example, Friedrich described the Allied bombing of German cities as *Vernichtung*, or annihilation, and referred to the crews of American and British bombers as *Einsatzgruppen*—the term used for the SS killing squads that operated behind German lines on the Eastern Front in World War II. This strategy, which Bill Niven has called "historical decontextualisation", implicitly equated the suffering caused by Germany and the suffering experienced by Germans during World War II.[24]

These collective memories of Germans as victims—above all of the bombing of Dresden in February 1945—both contributed to and fed on opposition to the US-led war in Iraq. During the build-up to the war, German television frequently showed images of the bombing of German cities during World War II, creating what Andreas Huyssen has called a "false sense of simultaneity" between the two conflicts.[25] The collective memory of the Allied bombings during World War II thus strengthened and intensified German opposition to the expected American war on Iraq.[26] Some Germans suggested that, having learned from their own terrible past, they were now in a better position than others to judge the justness of wars in the present. For example, Friedrich told the *Wall Street Journal* that "Germans have a deeper knowledge on matters of bombing campaigns."[27]

Thus, just as the debate in Germany about the Kosovo was informed by collective memories related to World War II, so was the debate about Iraq. However, in this case Germans were not perpetrators but victims—in particular, victims of the UK and the US. The discourse of German victimhood that was dominant in the Federal Republic in the 1950s had centred on the expulsion of Germans from central and Eastern European countries that became part of the Eastern Bloc after the war. But in the context of the Cold War, discussion of German suffering in which the perceived "perpetrators" were British and American—for example in Allied bombing of German cities during World War II—remained largely taboo except on the far right and the far left. That changed around the Millennium. In particular, for the first time, Germans were able to think of themselves as victims of Americans.

Some had thought that it was inevitable that, as time passed, memories of the Nazi past and World War II would simply recede. In fact, however, what happened in the 2000s was something more complex. The past did not simply recede as a factor in German public life, especially not in foreign policy. In fact, collective memories from World War II remained as powerful as ever. Rather, the balance between different collective memories from this period shifted as Germans seemed increasingly to think of themselves as victims as well as perpetrators. Both sets of collective memories could be mobilised according to the needs of the present. In particular, at the beginning of the twenty-first century, debates about German national identity were expressed through a competition between two specific collective memories: Auschwitz and Dresden.[28]

Around this time, the concept of "normality" also began to be used in debates about German foreign policy in a different way than during the previous decade.[29] Schröder had already justified German involvement in the Kosovo War, using the language of "normality". But at that time, he had adopted the right's definition of "normality" as *Bündnisfähigkeit*. For example, in a speech at the Munich Security Conference in February 1999, Schröder had said Germany did not want to pursue a *Sonderweg* and was ready to take responsibility "as a normal ally".[30] However, in the 2002 election, a number of Social Democrats also spoke of Germany's opposition to the Iraq War as an expression of "normality". For example, Parliamentary Leader Franz Müntefering declared in October 2002 that Germany was now a "normal country" that self-confidently pursued its interests—a rather different version of "normality".[31]

As Schröder was the first chancellor who did not have memories of 1945, his use of the language of "normality" is often explained in generational terms, even though other members of his generation such as Fischer rejected the concept of "normality". In fact, the person who made the left-wing case for a "normal" foreign policy first and most explicitly was Egon Bahr, who belonged to a quite different generation than Schröder: born in 1922, he was old enough to have served in the Wehrmacht at the end of World War II. But as Brandt's former foreign-policy adviser and the architect of the *Ostpolitik*, Bahr was an influential figure in German foreign-policy debates and someone whom Schröder acknowledged as a major influence.[32] It was Bahr who first formulated this new version of "normality" as the pursuit of the national interest.

In an essay in the foreign-policy journal *Internationale Politik* in January 1999, Bahr had called for a "normalisation of German politics".[33] He began the essay by welcoming Martin Walser's controversial Frankfurt speech, which had been delivered a few months earlier, and endorsed his criticism of the "instrumentalisation" of Auschwitz. In particular, Bahr argued that the Holocaust should not "block the road to normality" and "the stigma of the past should not weigh upon the future."[34] In effect, Bahr was directly applying the idea of the *Schlußstrich* to foreign policy: German foreign policy had to escape the "stigma" of the Nazi past in order to become "normal". This was an implicit critique of Joschka Fischer's Holocaust-centred view of German foreign policy.

The question, Bahr said, was whether Germany could attain an "inner balance" that would enable it to "act like other nations in the community of states" and whether "this normality will be understood and accepted by other nations."[35] He went on to explain what this "normality" meant in foreign-policy terms. The *Westbindung* and the European Union, which had resolved the "German question" once and for all, meant Germany was no longer a threat to the rest of Europe. Germany should therefore "pursue its interests in the same natural way as other sovereign states. This would be normality—"the opportunity of the Berlin Republic".[36] The implication of Bahr's essay was that the foreign policy of the Bonn Republic was "abnormal" not because it was reluctant to use military force but because it was not fully sovereign—a subtle but important difference.

Bahr also argued that the interests of Germany and the United States had now diverged, and thus identified "normality" with greater distance from the US. In other words, he was calling for the loosening of the *Westbindung* that some on the left like Jürgen Habermas had feared after unification. Whereas the earlier idea of "normality" as *Bündnisfähigkeit* was used to justify foreign-policy choices that coincided with those of Germany's NATO allies, such as choices made regarding the Kosovo War and the deployment of troops to Afghanistan, this new idea of "normality" as the pursuit of national interests could also be used to justify foreign-policy divergence from allies and especially from the US, such as its rejection of the Iraq War.

Although some Social Democrats like Müntefering had used the concept of "normality" in this way, as we have seen, Schröder's idea of a "German way" inevitably evoked the *Sonderweg*—in other words the opposite of "normality".[37] After he left office, Schröder said that although the phrase was meant above all to refer to the social market economy and was thus a critique of the "Anglo-Saxon economic model", it was also connected to foreign policy and in particular included a "reference to Brandt's peace policy".[38] But, after the first use of the term in his speech in Hanover in August 2002, Schröder tended to emphasise the social and economic rather than the foreign-policy element of the phrase.

In a book published after the war in 2003, Bahr picked up Schröder's idea of a "German way" in foreign policy and linked it directly to the idea of "normality". In *Der Deutsche Weg: Selbstverständlich und Normal*, he called for "a Germany in the service of Europe that pursues its interests as a normal state and does not let its future be impeded by its past: Europe's future is more important than Germany's past."[39] Once again, as in his earlier essay, "normality"—defined as the pursuit of national interests—was a central concept. Bahr argued that a sense of national identity was "normal" and that Germany suffered from a kind of deficit of national identity. "Germans have almost an obligation to develop a similarly normal relationship to the idea of the nation," he wrote.[40]

While criticising German exceptionalism based on the Nazi past as he had in his 1999 essay, Bahr now also placed greater emphasis than he had then on the need for a specifically German component of foreign policy. In particular, he identified "normality" with "singularity"—in other words, a specific national approach. Not only did he endorse Schröder's concept of a "German way", but he also said that he regretted the way Schröder had restricted the phrase to social and economic, rather than foreign, policy as a result of what he called a "fear of singularity".[41] Bahr urged Germans to overcome their "fear of the German way".[42] Other European countries, he said, were proud of the particularities of their own ways. "It is only the Germans who fear that others fear the German way that is no longer to be feared."[43]

In particular, Bahr argued that Germany should go its own way on the question of the use of military force. Article 26 of the Basic Law was a positive element of German "singularity" that could become a "unique selling point" on the basis of which Germany could develop its own distinctive foreign and security policy.[44] With this defence of Germany's reluctance to use military force, Bahr brought the concept of "normality" full circle from its original usage in the early 1990s. At that time, the right had argued that "normality" meant convergence with NATO allies on the question of the use of military force, and the left saw in this a danger of "remilitarisation". A decade later, however, Bahr argued that "normality" meant above all peace. By reconciling "normality" with "singularity", Bahr used the concept of "normality" to defend a kind of German exceptionalism—though a different kind than Fischer's.

Bahr argued again, as he had in 1999, that Germany's national interests—which formed the basis of a "normal" foreign policy—were no longer aligned with those of the US. "There are now different interests on either side of the Atlantic and they will remain different," he wrote.[45] If Germany did not end the dominance of the United States over its foreign and security policy, it would be nothing more than a protectorate.[46] Furthermore, Germany's identity as a *Friedensmacht*, or "force for peace"—its unique selling point—would help distinguish it from the US. Thus Bahr began the book by admitting: "I can see an upside to the Iraq War."[47] Later in the book, he suggested that the Iraq War helped unite Germans: "The reaction to the Iraq War was pan-German."[48]

Bahr's vision of a "normal" German foreign policy was thus a realist one based on the concept of sovereignty in which Germany above all pursued its own national interests. He argued that Germany should neither be influenced by Auschwitz as it had been in the 1990s nor be afraid to go its own way—especially when it stood for peace. Indeed, reluctance to use military force was the essence of its "singularity". Moreover, it should also stand apart from, and be prepared to challenge, the United States, particularly on the question of the use of military force. Although the discourse of "normality" had gone together with a resurgence of nationalism as some such as Habermas had feared, it did not go hand-in-hand with a resurgence of militarism. Rather, what emerged was a kind of left-wing nationalism based on the idea of Germany as a *Friedensmacht*.

After the Iraq War, others in Germany increasingly used the new version of the concept of "normality" that Bahr had formulated and came to share his vision of German foreign policy. In particular, although Schröder preferred to speak of "sovereignty" rather than "normality", he shared Bahr's realist emphasis on the pursuit of Germany's national interests.[49] Schröder agreed with Bahr that the Nazi past should not be used to justify German foreign-policy choices, and criticised Fischer's references to Auschwitz to justify military intervention in Kosovo.[50] He also said he did not regret the estrangement with the US and was proud of the way that his government had "claimed independence" in decision making.[51] Thus there emerged an updated version of the centre-left realism of the 1970s—now centred not on reunification but on what Bahr called "internal sovereignty".

Central to this centre-left realist foreign policy—as it was to that of Brandt in the 1970s—was the concept of "peace". The peace movement in the 1980s, which emerged in opposition to the deployment of US missiles in Europe, had already shown how much the concept of "peace" resonated in West Germany. The concept also resonated among East Germans. Under pressure from its allies in the 1990s, however, Germany had appeared to gradually reconcile itself to the use of military force under some circumstances. This shift in German security policy culminated in Germany's involvement in the Kosovo War in 1999. By the mid-2000s, German troops were deployed around the world. But particularly following the Iraq War in 2003, opposition in Germany to the use of military force increased and Germany began to define itself as a *Friedensmacht*.

German troops were playing a particularly active role in the Balkans. Although Kosovo had been stabilised, the ethnic conflicts in the region had by 2001 spread to neighbouring Macedonia, where fighting had broken out between ethnic Albanian paramilitaries and the government. In July 2001, after a ceasefire was agreed in Macedonia, NATO sent troops to the country to collect weapons from the Albanian rebels in Operation Essential Harvest. The following month, Germany agreed to contribute 500 soldiers as part of the 4,500-strong British-led mission. At the end of the thirty-day operation, it was Joschka Fischer who—just a few days before September 11—urged the United States and Europe to create a new NATO-led force with a United Nations mandate to keep Macedonia from descending further into civil war.[52]

German troops were also in Afghanistan, where Chancellor Schröder had deployed them in the name of *Bündnistreue*. But the mandate they were under, which had to be renewed every year, remained unclear. In particular, while the Bundeswehr was able to take part in the NATO-led ISAF force, it was not permitted to participate in the US-led anti-terror Operation Enduring Freedom—even though it was in practice difficult to separate the two operations. Following the rift over Iraq, Germany was no longer able to resist US pressure to make a greater contribution in Afghanistan, and in 2003 agreed to deploy troops to Kunduz in the relatively peaceful north of Afghanistan. According to Stefan Kornelius, the foreign editor of the *Süddeutsche Zeitung*, Germany agreed to do so because it was "the ideal place where the German interpretation of the mandate and the situation on the ground were in at least some kind of harmony".[53]

However, even there, the Bundeswehr operated under strict "caveats", which meant its troops could not be deployed with the same flexibility as those of their ISAF partners. While German officials are uncomfortable with the term "caveats" and prefer to talk of "rules of engagement", they admit that Germany had higher safety standards—for example in terms of the medical back-up that was required for troops to deploy—than other NATO countries, which restricted their ability to deploy. In practice, German commanders also took fewer risks than their American, British or Dutch counterparts, which placed restrictions on their forces' capabilities, particularly at night. These restrictions frustrated Germany's allies and led one senior British officer to quip in 2007 that the Bundeswehr was no more than an "aggressive camping organisation".[54]

However, from 2007 a process of adaptation and learning took place as the Bundeswehr struggled to deal with the operational challenges it faced in the north of the country. In particular, after the Taliban opened a second front in the north of Afghanistan and the security situation there deteriorated, German commanders were forced to change the way they operated and began to adopt a more aggressive force posture. In the process, the Bundeswehr, which until then had seen its role in terms of peacekeeping operations, began to develop its own counter-insurgency doctrine. But that in turn increased the disconnect between the reality on the ground and what Timo Noetzel has called "strategic inertia" at the political level as public opposition to German involvement in the ISAF mission increased.[55]

As German and civilian casualties increased, opposition to the mission in Afghanistan hardened. Research carried out by the Bundeswehr suggests that from 2007—that is, when German boots were on the ground in the north of Afghanistan—Germans became more sceptical about the ISAF mission in particular and about the deployment of German troops abroad in general.[56] Politicians avoided discussing the deployment of the Bundeswehr in Afghanistan, which was usually referred to as a "stabilisation operation"—not least because of fears that it could be used by political opponents in the way that Schröder had used Iraq. Stefan Kornelius wrote in the summer of 2009 that Germany had deceived itself about what it was doing in Afghanistan. "Although Germany is fighting a war, one is not allowed to call it a war," he wrote.[57]

Later that year, however, the reality of Afghanistan caught up with Germany. In the run-up to the general election in 2009, German troops in the north of the country came under greater pressure from Taliban attacks. On 4 September, a German colonel called in a US air strike on two oil tankers in Kunduz that were believed to have been hijacked by the Taliban.[58] The incident, in which dozens of civilians were killed, led later to the resignation of Labour Minister Franz Josef Jung, who had been defence minister at the time of the air strike and had given incomplete information about it. The Kunduz incident came to transform German attitudes to the mission in Afghanistan. The ensuing debate made many Germans finally realise that the Bundeswehr was fighting a war rather than simply taking part in a "stabilisation operation".[59]

In addition to the trauma of Afghanistan, the perceived failure of the Iraq War reinforced opposition to involvement of German troops in "out-of-area" operations. In fact, by the end of the second decade after reunification, "Never again war" seemed to have replaced "Never again Auschwitz" as Germany's guiding principle on the use of military force. "The interventionist episode in German foreign and security policy seems to be over," wrote the journalist Thomas Schmid in 2010.[60] But while some in Europe increasingly saw Germany as a consumer rather than a producer of security, Germany saw itself as a fundamentally peaceful, "post-heroic" society that was no longer interested in power projection. Thus, whereas in the 1990s it seemed as if Germany was converging with France and the UK on the use of military force, it now seemed as if Germany was diverging from them. In matters of war and peace, it seemed, Germans did not want to be "normal".

5

ECONOMICS AND POLITICS

As German national identity underwent a shift in the 2000s, a transformation was also taking place in the German economy that would have huge consequences for the rest of Europe. As Germany struggled to deal with the enormous cost of reunification and, simultaneously, with the challenge of globalisation, it undertook difficult reforms that led to an extraordinary economic revival but also changed Germany and its previously symbiotic relationship with the rest of the EU. At the centre of the increasingly integrated eurozone, Germany went, in a decade, from a current account deficit to a huge surplus. Within Germany the turnaround was seen as a triumph. But because it was achieved largely through wage restraint, ordinary Germans did not feel they had benefited from it. Furthermore, since it made Germany much more dependent on exports, it created tensions within Europe.

The initial effect of reunification in 1990, as in the case of unification in 1871, was to produce an economic boom. Wages in the east, which at the time of reunification were only around 60 per cent of those in West Germany, were quickly brought up to western levels, which created a new market of 17 million people with money in their pockets to spend on West German products. Thus in the first year after reunification, the West German economy grew by 4.5 per cent as it responded to the new demand. The construction industry in particular felt the effects of the improved economy, as the German government massively invested in infrastructure in the so-called "new states" of the former East Germany as part of a programme called *Aufschwung Ost*. Berlin—where the government was set to move in 1999—was reconstructed as the new capital of the reunified Germany.

However, as the initial euphoria of reunification passed, economic problems began to emerge that would dominate German politics for the next decade. As the initial surge in consumer demand in the east passed and uncompetitive factories previously owned by the East German state were sold off or shut down and output fell, the German economy plunged into recession. The economy grew by only 1.1 per cent in 1992 and shrank by 1.1 per cent in 1993. The Federal Republic, which until then had run an almost continuous current-account surplus since the early 1950s, went into deficit. During the election campaign in 1990, Kohl had promised "blooming landscapes" in the former GDR. But by 1993, 15 per cent of the workforce in the "new states" was unemployed. Prospects, especially for young people, seemed to be diminishing rather than improving.

During the final years of the Kohl government, as growth remained sluggish, unemployment increased and the welfare state was overstretched, there was much talk of a *Reformstau*, or reform logjam. Many economists thought of Germany as the "sick man of Europe": it was too dependent on manufacturing and had an inflexible labour market, and therefore could not compete with lower-cost industries in China and Eastern Europe. They thought Germany should deregulate its economy and seek more growth from financial services and consumer spending, which was low compared to other, similarly developed economies. But Germany's consensus system of government, and in particular its strong trade unions, seemed to make it "unreformable". However, under Gerhard Schröder in the 2000s, a remarkable and unexpected turnaround took place that, according to Barry Eichengreen, was the product of a mixture of "good policy and good luck".[1]

When he came to power in 1998, Schröder sought above all to reduce unemployment, which stood at 3.7 million, or just over 9 per cent. It had been rising as Germany struggled to cope with reunification and as Germany's previously successful manufacturers faced increasing competition from Japan and other Asian economies. Schröder had come to power promising economic renewal after the stagnation of the Kohl era. In fact, on taking office, he had gone so far as to say he did not deserve to be re-elected if he did not significantly reduce unemployment. He promised a more business-friendly economic policy—based on what his adviser Bodo Hombach called a "supply-side economics of the left"—that would help to stimulate Germany's sluggish economy.[2]

In his first term, Schröder almost completely failed to overcome Germany's *Reformstau*. Preoccupied by foreign-policy crises such as Kosovo, Afghanistan and Iraq, he was distracted from the economy. The first few months of his administration were chaotic as he feuded with his finance minister and party leader, Oskar Lafontaine, who wanted to increase taxes and stimulate demand. After Lafontaine suddenly resigned in March 1999, his replacement, Hans Eichel, made severe spending cuts. Nevertheless, the economic data went from bad to worse. In fact, at the end of Schröder's first term, unemployment stood at nearly 3.5 million, or just under 9 per cent. But in his second term, between 2002 and 2005, Schröder introduced the biggest reform of the German social security system since the Federal Republic began, which transformed the German economy.

The most significant set of measures was a package of reforms introduced in March 2003 known as Agenda 2010 that cut unemployment and health care benefits and reduced state pensions. Most controversially, it included a reform of unemployment benefit based on recommendations by Peter Hartz, the personnel director of Volkswagen, whom Schröder had appointed as the head of a commission to modernise the labour market just before the election in 2002. (Hartz was subsequently forced to resign when it emerged that he had been involved in a massive corruption scandal involving paying kickbacks to union bosses and even paying for prostitutes for them.) The reforms also made it easier for very small companies to fire employees and eliminated social security contributions on earnings of less than €400 a month, which helped reduce unit-labour costs and thus encouraged the creation of part-time jobs.

The measures were attacked from both the left and right. While some such as the Council of Economic Experts—the "five wise men" who advise the German government on economic policy—thought the measures did not go far enough in reforming Germany's overstretched welfare state, many on the left saw them as neo-liberal or even Thatcherite. In particular, they had increased the gap between rich and poor and created a new underclass of low-paid and part-time workers. Led by the powerful trade unions, opponents of "Hartz IV", as the reforms of unemployment benefit were known, began protesting. In the east, where the reforms had an especially significant impact, disillusioned voters turned to the PDS, the party that had grown out of the East German Communist party. Furthermore, the Schröder reforms did not immediately have a positive impact on the German economy.[3] Growth remained slow and unemployment—the self-imposed test of Schröder's government—continued to rise. By the end of 2002 it had risen to 3.7 million, or over 9 per cent.

As a result of the dire economy, Germany struggled to maintain the limits on budget deficits to which it had committed in the Stability and Growth Pact (SGP). The pact had been created in 1997 on Germany's initiative to enforce the fiscal discipline required by the Masstricht Treaty. But in early 2003 it became clear that, the previous year, France and Germany had both exceeded the 3 per cent limit. However, in November, the Economic and Financial Affairs Council of the EU, consisting of member state finance ministers, rejected the European Commission's recommendation to continue taking further steps in the so-called excessive deficit procedure against them. Germany continued to violate the terms of the SGP—and thus, in effect, suspended it—until it was reformed in 2005. This fiscal pragmatism—the opposite of the fiscal discipline that Germany would later impose on others in Europe—contributed to Germany's economic success over the following decade.

Meanwhile, however, German manufacturing was undergoing a transformation of its own. Perhaps most importantly, German manufacturers began outsourcing production to central and Eastern Europe. Before reunification, the German economy had been largely cut off from these economies—once part of a German-centred *Mitteleuropa*—by the iron curtain. But the end of the Cold War suddenly created an arc of low-wage economies with skilled workers on Germany's borders. In the second half of the 2000s, German companies began to relocate production to countries such as the Czech Republic, Hungary, Poland and Slovakia—which had all acceded to the EU in 2004—to reduce costs and improve competitiveness. For example, the carmaker Audi, a subsidiary of Volkswagen, began producing its automobile engines in Hungary. In the twenty years from 1993, it invested €5.7 billion in Hungary and became the country's biggest foreign direct investor.[4]

This kind of outsourcing transformed German manufacturing. Increasingly, German-branded manufactured goods, including automobiles, were actually produced elsewhere and merely assembled in Germany. This was good for the economies of central Europe, which benefited from investment and training and the creation of jobs. But it also meant that much of central Europe became part of the German supply chain—integrated into what one economist calls a "greater German economy" that gave Germany an inbuilt competitiveness advantage relative to other eurozone economies.[5] It also aligned to a large extent the economic interests of these countries with those of Germany and thus increased German power within the EU.

Offshoring also did something else: it put downward pressure on wages of skilled workers within Germany. With unemployment rising, German trade unions, traditionally thought of as some of Europe's toughest, agreed to remarkable wage restraint. This was facilitated by the consensual system of corporate governance known as *Mitbestimmung*, or "co-determination". In particular, management and works councils used the tool of plant-level bargaining called "employment pacts", which had been introduced by Daimler Benz in the late 1980s, to reach agreements that aimed to improve the competitiveness of plants, and with it job security.[6] Both sides compromised: workers worked longer and accepted pay cuts and more flexible working patterns; management guaranteed investment and promised not to make mass redundancies.

As a result of such agreements, wages rose just 1.1 per cent a year in Germany in the 2000s—in other words, they were flat in real terms. According to an International Labour Organisation report, real earnings (that is, adjusted for inflation) actually fell by 4.5 per cent in the 2000s.[7] This wage restraint, together with the elimination of social security contributions on low-paid jobs that Schröder had introduced, led to a dramatic drop in unit labour costs in Germany at a time when they were increasing elsewhere in the eurozone. Thus a competitiveness gap opened up between Germany and other eurozone countries. For example, relative to the eurozone, price competitiveness increased by 10 per cent; relative to some countries such as Italy and Spain, it increased by 25 per cent.[8] But this relative increase in competitiveness was due to a fall in unit labour costs rather than productivity growth, which was actually higher in France.[9] In short, Adam Posen argues, Germany had "internally devalued its way to competitiveness".[10]

As a result of this internal devaluation, Germany bucked the trend among developed economies, which in the 2000s were seeing their share of the world export market decrease. As emerging economies increasingly competed with developed economies in world export markets, developed economies saw their share of these markets decline. But even as other European countries fell behind, German manufacturers managed to maintain their share of the world market and their share of Germany's GDP. The German manufacturing boom led to a dramatic turnaround in the economy. In the second half of the 2000s—that is, after Angela Merkel had succeeded Schröder as chancellor in 2005—unemployment began to fall from its peak of 4.8 million, or 11.5 per cent. As exports surged and domestic demand remained low, Germany went from a trade deficit of 1.7 per cent of GDP in 2000 to a surplus of 7.4 per cent in 2007.

However, the revival of manufacturing skewed the German economy. It had always been based on manufacturing and dependent on exports—indeed, many large and medium-sized companies had histories that went back to the nineteenth or early twentieth century. But as domestic demand remained low and manufacturers recovered in the 2000s, it became even more heavily dependent on exports than it had been until then. In fact, the contribution of exports to Germany's GDP went from 33 per cent in 2000 to 48 per cent in 2010.[11] By the end of the decade, the German economy was, as Simon Tilford has put it, "structurally reliant on foreign demand for its growth".[12] Germany's automobile industry was a microcosm of its economy as a whole: around the time of reunification, Germany had exported around half of the cars it produced; by the end of the 2000s it exported more than three-quarters of the cars it produced.[13]

The huge surplus produced by this combination of low domestic demand and surging exports needed to be invested somewhere. In the 1950s and 1960s, German companies had tended to invest at home. But, in part because of high taxes in Germany and in part because of the emergence of more lucrative opportunities outside the country, when Germany returned to surplus in the 2000s they tended to invest elsewhere. Thus Germany's surplus "circled the world", as Raghuram Rajan has put it, before being invested in property in Ireland and Spain and in mortgage-backed securities in the US—so-called subprime.[14] And thus the surplus produced by wage restraint in Germany was recycled into "over-sized exposures to junk foreign securities".[15] Meanwhile, as Adam Tooze has pointed out, net investment in Germany as a share of GDP was lower than at any time in recorded history apart from during the

Great Depression.[16] Germany was, Adam Posen argues, moving "down the value chain in relative terms, not up".[17]

The German economy that emerged from internal devaluation that took place during the Schröder era was therefore one that was successful but also fragile. Many Germans had kept their jobs in manufacturing even as their employers faced greater competition from emerging economies. But because the improvement in competitiveness had been achieved largely through wage restraint, ordinary Germans did not feel they had benefited from the so-called second *Wirtschaftswunder*, or economic miracle. This in turn kept domestic demand low. The low rate of public and private investment also did not bode well for productivity growth in the medium-term. While manufacturing had adapted, services had hardly been liberalised at all. Perhaps most importantly, the German economy was fragile because it was so dependent on external demand—and therefore vulnerable to external shocks.

This, in the 2000s, is where luck came in. As Germany underwent difficult structural reforms under Schröder, it benefited from a buoyant global economy. The US cut interest rates to historic lows to stimulate the economy after the dot-com bubble burst and emerging economies continued to grow rapidly, which meant demand for German exports remained high. As a result, even as the German state cut benefits and companies cut wages, the economy was able to grow. It was also helped by the creation of the euro, which produced a credit boom in the eurozone and, since it was weak compared to the deutsche mark, benefited German exports beyond the eurozone. However, although this meant there was a boom for German exporters, the credit boom created problems that would eventually lead to conflict.

After the creation of the single currency, the risk premiums on the government bonds of countries such as Greece "melted away", as the economist Paul Krugman put it.[18] Banks, including German ones, lent at historically low rates to the south of Europe, which went on a borrowing spree—and bought all kinds of German products, from luxury cars to the four Type 214 submarines purchased by the Greek government. By 2007, the Greek current account deficit was 15 per cent of GDP.[19] Meanwhile, Germany's trade surplus with the rest of the eurozone grew dramatically. Between 1997 and 2007, it went from €28 billion to €109 billion—that is, it almost quadrupled. That in turn was recycled back into the south—in particular into construction and property in Spain.

What had happened since the creation of the euro, we now know, was that the imbalances between eurozone economies, especially between countries with trade surpluses (such as Germany) and countries with trade deficits (such as Greece), had grown. This was the opposite of what was supposed to happen in the EU and the eurozone in particular. The idea of the single currency was that while countries such as Greece would emulate Germany's low-inflation, low interest rate model, Germany would conversely also move closer to their model by increasing domestic spending, wages and inflation.[20] "The structural differences between a low-inflation, slow growing core and higher inflation periphery were supposed to narrow following the introduction of the single currency," Simon Tilford wrote. "In reality, these differences grew."[21] In short, instead of producing convergence, the euro had produced divergence.

In particular, the huge size of the German surplus became a problem. The eurozone could cope with a small economy with a current-account surplus of 6 or 7 per cent as a proportion of GDP. For example, the Netherlands had an even bigger current-account surplus as a proportion of GDP than Germany. But, as Tilford argued in a prescient report in 2006, an economy as big as Germany's could not "depend indefinitely on exports to drive real GDP growth without imposing intolerable pressures on other members of EMU".[22] In the first decade after the creation of the euro, however, there was little awareness of these emerging pressures and the new currency seemed to be a huge success. The fears that some had at the time of its introduction were largely forgotten as the euro seemed to be on the verge of becoming a global reserve currency to rival the dollar.

At the same time as this surge in demand for German goods from within Europe, global demand was also increasing. As emerging economies developed and the global middle class expanded, demand for technology and consumer goods exploded. Germany, which specialised in sectors such as machinery, automobiles, electrical goods and chemicals, was ideally placed to benefit. In particular, there was huge demand for two types of German goods. First, the expansion and development of industrial production created demand for capital goods at which Germany excelled, such as machine tools. Second, the expansion of the middle class created demand for premium goods such as luxury automobiles. There was an almost perfect symbiosis between Germany and many emerging economies. "We have exactly the products they need," said one German official in 2012.[23]

It was above all from China that demand increased. The symbiosis was even more perfect than with other emerging economies because the Chinese state wanted to move up the manufacturing value chain and needed technology to do so. In the 2000s, big German companies such as BASF and Volkswagen began setting up plants in China. By the end of the decade China had become the biggest market for the S-Class, Mercedes's most profitable vehicle, and by 2013 would account for half of total worldwide sales.[24] The *Mittelstand*—the medium-sized German companies, many family-owned, with fewer than 500 employees and annual sales of less than €50 million that contributed 60 per cent of Germany's jobs and half the country's GDP—also benefited. Both those supplying other German exporters and those directly supplying Chinese companies boomed on the back of demand from China. The only problem was finding enough skilled workers to cope.

Just as the euro helped demand from within the eurozone by creating cheap credit, so it helped make German companies more competitive in key markets outside Europe, such as Asia and the US. Before the creation of the euro, German exporters had struggled with the strength of the deutsche mark. But they now benefited from the weakness of the euro relative to deutsche mark, which made their products much more competitive beyond Europe. Although it is impossible to know what the exchange rate of the deutsche mark against the dollar would have been in the 2000s if the euro had not been created, it would certainly have been stronger than the euro was, which would have made German exports more expensive. Thus to some critics, German exporters were benefiting unfairly from an undervalued currency; Germany was therefore not only benefiting from demand from China but also itself becoming "the China of Europe".[25]

As the German economy became increasingly dependent on demand from beyond Europe, German foreign policy seemed to become more realist. The paradigmatic case during Schröder's time in office was Germany's relationship with Russia. After Schröder and President Vladimir Putin had joined forces to oppose the Iraq War, the two men developed an ever-closer personal relationship and Schröder described Putin as a "flawless democrat" despite his increasing authoritarianism. Two weeks before the election in 2005, Schröder and Putin signed a deal to build a gas pipeline from Russia to Germany, which would make

Germany the main distributor of Russian gas in Europe while increasing Europe's dependence on Russia. Just two months after leaving office, Schröder was appointed as the chairman of the board of Nord Stream, the consortium set up to build the pipeline, which was majority-owned by the Russian energy company Gazprom. Even after Russia invaded Georgia in 2008, Schröder refused to say a bad word about Russia.[26]

Much of German policy towards Russia was driven by business, especially the energy sector. By the time of the Russo-Georgian War, trade between Germany and Russia had grown to $50 billion with German exports to Russia totalling $36 billion. Germany also depended on Russia for 37 per cent of its gas—which Russia under Putin increasingly used as a political weapon—and 32 per cent of its oil. German companies like E.ON Ruhrgas, Gazprom's partner in Nord Stream, opposed attempts to liberalise the European gas market in order to reduce dependence on Russia. The stakeholders in the relationship with Russia were largely in the economic community and represented by the Ost-Ausschuß der Deutschen Wirtschaft, or Committee on Eastern European Economic Relations—a powerful lobby that exercised a significant influence on German policy towards Russia.[27] Influential analysts such as Alexander Rahr said it was Germany's "destiny" to have a "special relationship" with Russia.[28]

At the same time, Germany was also developing an increasingly close relationship with China—potentially an even more important economic partner than Russia. Schröder made a point of visiting China at least once a year in order to promote German exporters, particularly automakers.[29] This led to a number of big contracts, including a $1.5 billion project involving Siemens and ThyssenKrupp to build a high-speed magnetic levitation railway line in Shanghai (although the project was only partially completed). Meanwhile, Schröder remained conspicuously silent about human rights abuses by the Chinese government. He took what he called a more "patient" approach to human rights in China based on "persistent communication" rather than "punitive measures": rather than argue about human rights abuses, German and Chinese officials would discuss the rule of law.[30] Schröder also supported lifting the EU's embargo on selling arms to China, which had been in place since the Tiananmen Square massacre in 1989.

When Angela Merkel took over from Schröder in 2005, initially at the head of a "grand coalition" of Christian Democrats and Social Democrats, she promised to return to a values-based foreign policy. In particular, she pledged in 2006 to show "courage to take a more critical tone" towards China.[31] The following year she received the Dalai Lama in the chancellery, which led to a crisis in relations between Beijing and Berlin. Foreign Minister Frank-Walter Steinmeier—who had previously been Schröder's chief of staff—sought to bring the standoff with China to an end by sending a confidential letter to his Chinese counterpart on the issue of Tibet. The letter has never been made public, but it has been reported that in it Steinmeier recognised that Tibet was "part of Chinese territory"—a more precise statement of Germany's "one China policy" than in the past. The Chinese state media saw this as a diplomatic victory.[32]

However, after the crisis was over, Merkel seemed to revert to the export-driven foreign policy that had begun under Schröder. Although she did not get along with Putin as well as Schröder, and was more cautious in her approach to Russia than he was, she nevertheless pressed ahead with Nord Stream, opposed extending NATO membership to Ukraine or Georgia, and pursued a "partnership for modernisation" with Russia. Merkel also began visiting China once a year as Schröder had done, and increasingly appeared to tone down public criticism on human rights—what a member of the Bundestag's foreign relations committee called a "new realism".[33] Chinese analysts and officials would later say that Merkel had "understood", become "more careful" and learned "where the red lines are".[34]

During Schröder's time in office, the chancellery had become more active in promoting the interests of business, for example, by bringing large trade delegations on visits abroad. One German journalist later wrote that the foreign ministry and its 230 embassies around the world increasingly saw themselves as "service providers for the export industry".[35] Because many of the emerging economies on which Germany increasingly depended were authoritarian states in which the state owned large sections of the economy, German companies needed the help of German officials to secure contracts. German politicians, in turn, needed companies to produce jobs. Thus, driven by economic interests, Germany developed an increasingly close relationship with authoritarian powers around the world such as China and Russia.

The inspiration for this new export-driven foreign policy—particularly among Social Democrats such as Schröder and Steinmeier—was *Ostpolitik*. *Ostpolitik* was still seen in Germany as one of the Federal Republic's big foreign-policy successes—a decisive and distinctively West German contribution to the end of the Cold War. In fact, many in Germany thought that it was détente, rather than more aggressive US policies, that had brought the Cold War to an end. The lesson for future policy that many in Germany drew was that, as Stephen Szabo has put it, "dialogue, diplomacy, mutual trust and multilateralism were the best approaches for dealing with seemingly intractable opponents."[36] *Ostpolitik* had become a kind of model for German diplomats. The German foreign-policy establishment talked endlessly about the need for co-operation rather confrontation with authoritarian powers like China and Russia.

However, the policy Germany increasingly pursued towards authoritarian powers was in reality quite different from *Ostpolitik*. *Ostpolitik* had been conceived during the Cold War as a way to bring about reunification through a policy of small steps, not to transform the Soviet Union. Egon Bahr had sought détente with the Soviet Union through the "weaving" of political and cultural ties between West and East Germany—not just trade. *Ostpolitik* had been based on the idea of *Wandel durch Annäherung*, or change through rapprochement. But at some point, *Wandel durch Annäherung* had become reduced to *Wandel durch Handel*, or "change through trade". The hope was simply that, as Schröder put it, "economic exchange" would lead to "societal change".[37] It was a slogan that could be used to justify business as usual under almost any circumstances—in effect, a policy of no red lines.

A striking example of Germany's new realist foreign policy was its approach to Iran. After it emerged in 2002 that Iran was enriching uranium at two secret facilities and the International Atomic Energy Agency (IAEA) launched an investigation, it was above all China and Russia that made it so hard for the West to impose tougher economic sanctions on Iran. But Germany, the largest Western exporter to Iran and the third largest overall, was also initially reluctant to confront Iran because of the economic ties between the countries. Because of the leverage it had through these ties, Germany was invited to the E3+3 negotiations and eventually supported tougher sanctions after Merkel took over as chancellor. But at no point did Germany lead Europe, let alone the West, in attempts to get tougher sanctions.

The case of Iran also illustrated how the Holocaust had receded in importance in German foreign-policy debates since Fischer had been accused of "instrumentalising" Auschwitz in the debate about Kosovo. Although the Iranian regime was the world's most openly anti-Semitic since World War II, particularly under President Mahmoud Ahmadinejad, the Holocaust was almost entirely absent from the debate about the Iranian nuclear issue. Few suggested, for instance, that because of the Nazi past, Germany might have a special responsibility to prevent Iran acquiring nuclear weapons. Despite the strong current of opposition in Germany to nuclear power and nuclear weapons that went back to the 1980s peace movement, Germans seemed to fear war—for example in the form of an Israeli military strike on Iran—much more than the prospect of a nuclear-armed Iran.

This shift towards a more economically driven German foreign policy was a delayed consequence of the changed strategic environment in which Germany found itself after reunification. During the Cold War, as we have seen, the Federal Republic had above all sought rehabilitation and security. But since reunification, those two goals had been largely achieved; Germany was "strategically saturated", as the Free Democrat politician Alexander Graf Lambsdorff put it in a phrase that recalled Bismarck's idea of Germany as a "satiated power" after unification.[38] Thus German foreign policy became more economically driven almost by default—that is, in the absence of overriding strategic objectives. Meanwhile, as the challenges and costs of reunification and the competition created by globalisation brought about greater economic difficulties, the German government came under greater pressure to prioritise economic growth over other foreign-policy goals.

In particular, Germany no longer needed its traditional allies and partners in the way it did during the Cold War when it faced an existential threat from the Soviet Union. Above all, this had transformed the relationship between Germany and the United States. The rift with the US over the Iraq War had weakened the *Westbindung*. But even after Barack Obama became US president in 2008, the relationship between Germany and the US did not fully recover. In fact, though the new US president was even more popular in Germany than elsewhere in Europe, this popularity did not translate into any concessions towards the US on policy—for example on Afghanistan, to which the US wanted Germany to make a greater commitment.

Germany's relationship with the EU also cooled as enlargement made it harder for the former to get its own way. Under Schröder, Germany was more willing to pursue its own economic interests—as its violation of the Stability and Growth Pact illustrated. In May 2000 Joschka Fischer had argued in his Humboldt speech in Berlin for the "completion" of European integration—a speech that led to drafting of a new European Constitution. But the German public was becoming more Eurosceptic—and so was the judiciary. In a landmark decision in June 2009, the constitutional court approved the Lisbon Treaty—an attempt to streamline EU decision making even after the constitution was rejected by Dutch and French voters—but also imposed limits on the further transfer of sovereignty to Brussels in a long list of policy areas including security, fiscal, and social policy.[39]

Thus by the end of the 2000s, Germany's commitment to multilateralism—a key element of the Federal Republic's foreign policy—had somewhat weakened. This commitment had never been an altruistic one. Rather, the Federal Republic's multilateralism had been "attritional"—in other words, it was a way for a constrained power to gradually achieve its own foreign-policy ambitions and objectives, above all sovereignty and reunification.[40] But this approach had been so successful that, over the years, it had become a kind of reflex for the German foreign-policy establishment. During the 2000s, a shift from this "reflexive" multilateralism to a more "contingent" multilateralism took place: German politicians across the board now picked and chose when to use multilateral institutions. Thus Germany would operate through multilateral institutions when it suited it to do so and bilaterally when it did not.

As the case of Iran illustrated, Germany's new export-driven foreign policy also fitted neatly with Germany's growing reluctance to use military force. Since the 1990s, Western powers had increasingly sought to use military force where necessary to enforce international norms. In particular, the United Nations General Assembly had agreed the doctrine of a "responsibility to protect" in 2005, which had thus become part of international law. But such interventions—from Kosovo in 1999 to Afghanistan in 2011—were seen as a kind of "new imperialism" in countries such as China.[41] Germany could justify its opposition to the use of military force in the name of "peace"; but avoiding taking part in military interventions also enabled Germany to avoid disputes over values or even security issues that might get in the way of doing business—particularly with sovereigntist powers beyond Europe that opposed liberal interventionism.

Thus in the 2000s, Germany seemed to go from a "civilian power" to a mere "trading state". The overriding foreign-policy objective of a civilian power, as we have seen, is to civilise international relations through the development of the international rule of law. In particular, by avoiding the use of force except collectively and with international legitimacy, a civilian power aims to help develop a multilateral monopoly on the use of force analogous to the state's domestic monopoly. But in the 2000s, as its economy became increasingly dependent on exports, Germany's objectives seemed to narrow from the civilisation of international relations to the pursuit of its own prosperity. To many Germans, this was something to be proud of. In fact, this economic focus seemed to them to show how much of a break with the past Germany had made.

If the Iraq War was the critical juncture that had given Germans the confidence to go their own way on matters of war and peace, the financial crisis that began in the autumn of 2008 with the collapse of Lehman Brothers gave them confidence to do so on economic issues as well. Germans saw it above all as a crisis of Anglo-Saxon capitalism. In fact, though the crisis had begun in the US, German banks such as Deutsche Bank and Commerzbank, as well as the Landesbanken (the banks owned by German states) had also been involved in subprime lending and, it would later emerge, had made bad loans in southern Europe too. Nevertheless, to many Germans, particularly on the left, the crisis demonstrated how wrong the UK and the US were to focus on the "new economy" and on financial services. They saw in the crisis a vindication of the German social market economy with its focus on the real economy and on exports.

The crisis also produced a rejection of Keynesianism—which Germans associated with Anglo-Saxon economists. The Social Democrat finance minister at the time of the crisis, Peer Steinbrück, saw the crisis as one caused by "credit-financed growth". In 2009 the grand coalition had already introduced a so-called *Schuldenbremse*, or debt brake, which amended the German constitution to set a limit on the government budget deficit. The constitutional amendment committed the federal government to cut its structural deficit (that is, adjusted for the business cycle) to 0.35 per cent of GDP by 2016 and the sixteen states to eliminate their structural deficit entirely by 2020. Some German economists had thought it was "madness", but they were a minority.[42] The crisis further strengthened what Adam Tooze has called Germany's "anti-debt consensus".[43]

This anti-Keynesian turn in Germany led to furious disagreements with other Western countries about how to "rebalance" the global economy that foreshadowed the debates that would take place after the euro crisis began. Many Anglo-Saxon economists thought that the crisis was a Keynesian moment—as Paul Krugman put it, "essentially the same kind of situation that John Maynard Keynes described back in the 1930s".[44] The problem was a lack of aggregate demand, which meant that stimulus was required. But as finance minister in December 2008, the Social Democrat Peer Steinbrück attacked the "crass Keynesianism" of the British government under Gordon Brown, who had urged stimulus measures.[45] That in turn prompted an angry response from Krugman, who called the German government "boneheaded".[46]

In fact, despite his criticism of Brown, Steinbrück subsequently introduced stimulus measures of his own, including a version of the US "cash for clunkers" programme, which boosted car sales in Germany, and a "short work" scheme, which kept German autoworkers in work even as the economy slowed. Partly as a result of these measures, and because of demand from China—itself the result of the four trillion yuan ($586 billion) Chinese stimulus—the German economy recovered rapidly. But to many Germans, the success of the German economy in bouncing back from the crisis illustrated German virtues rather than a recovery of the world economy. For example, Michael Glos, a former Christian Democrat economics minister, later said it was no "miracle" that Germany had got through the crisis so well. "We stuck to manufacturing whereas other countries deindustrialized."[47]

In March 1990, as we have seen, Jürgen Habermas had worried about the emergence of "DM nationalism". Shortly afterwards, Germany agreed to give up the deutsche mark for the euro. But as the German economy recovered, and particularly after the economic crisis, Germany's economic nationalism appeared to re-emerge in another form. This new version of economic nationalism centred on Germany's world-beating exports, which had seemed to replace the deutsche mark as the symbol of German economic success. Germany had always been proud of being an *Exportweltmeister*—a term that implied it was the winner of a contest. But in the 2000s exports seemed to become central not just to the German economy but also to German national identity itself: Germans increasingly thought of themselves as an *Exportnation*, or export nation.

Even if Germany's opposition to the Iraq War, and in particular Schröder's unilateral approach, had not undermined Germany's claim to be a "civilian power", the way that Germany increasingly defined its national interest in economic terms, and specifically in terms of exports, did. Using economic rather than military means to civilise international relations through the development of the international rule of law was something quite different to the pursuit of economic objectives and, above all, the promotion of exports—which was more reminiscent of the mercantilism of nineteenth century great powers, albeit without the use of military force. Hanns Maull, the theorist of Germany as a "civilian power", would later write that Germany's "obsession" with exports had eroded its civilian power identity.[48]

Thus at the end of the 2000s there was once again a triumphalist mood in Germany. In particular, there was an increasing scepticism about—and even contempt for—Anglo-Saxon ideas, whether about statecraft or about economics, which drew on a longer history of anti-Americanism in German thinking.[49] Germany seemed to have been proven right. It seemed to have done what would later be endlessly referred to as its "homework". Many argued that others in Europe and the rest of the world should now learn from it; thus the idea of "Modell Deutschland", which went back to the 1970s, re-emerged.[50] In fact, there was in this sense of German triumphalism, which had begun even before the euro crisis, something of the idea of a German mission—the idea expressed in Emmanuel Geibel's 1861 poem that "the essence of the German nation will one day be the world's salvation."

6

EUROPE AND THE WORLD

Much of Germany's response to the euro crisis can be explained by the changes that had taken place in the Federal Republic since reunification. By the beginning of 2010, Germany was after all a "different republic" to the one it had been before 1990—though not quite in the way that some had feared at that time. Its foreign policy had undergone a complex mixture of continuity and change. In the first decade after reunification, German strategic culture had seemed to converge with that of France and the UK as Germany reconciled itself to the idea of using military force, particularly as part of humanitarian interventions. But in the second decade after reunification, as collective memories in which Germans were victims increasingly competed with those in which Germans were perpetrators, opposition to the use of military force seemed once again to harden—though Germany was no longer able or willing to practice a kind of compensatory "chequebook diplomacy".

In 2010 Germany was a country that thought of itself as "normal" in the sense envisaged by Egon Bahr—a right-wing concept from the *Historikerstreit* that the left had, during the 2000s, adopted and adapted. A consensus had emerged, in part through the influence of centre-left politicians such as Bahr as well as right-wing thinkers such as Nolte, that German foreign policy should no longer be "held hostage" to Auschwitz, as Helmut Schmidt had put it in 1981. There was a sense that Germany should be free, like other sovereign nation states, to articulate and pursue its own national interest—even where that meant diverging from its

Western allies and European partners. There was a revival of the idea of a distinct "German way"—an idea that went back to the beginning of German nationalism—that was, in particular, superior to the "American way" and Anglo-Saxon ideas on strategy and economics.

Politically, Germany was less constrained than it was before reunification, when it relied on the US and NATO for protection from the Soviet Union and on the EU as part of its post-war rehabilitation. Economically, however, it was more constrained than before reunification. Germany's world-beating manufacturers had come under increasing pressure from globalisation but during the 2000s had adapted and regained competitiveness. Although it was largely the result of wage restraint and the favourable external environment, Germans were proud of their success as an exporter. But Germany's export nationalism was also part of what made it so difficult for Germany to resolve the euro crisis. In particular, by the time the crisis began, Germany's extreme dependence on exports for economic growth had created a tension in its foreign-policy priorities between Europe and the rest of the world.

The Greek crisis that began in 2010 thrust Germany into an extraordinary—and, in the history of the EU, unprecedented—position. As the biggest creditor country in a crisis of a currency made up of sovereign states, it could impose conditions on debtor countries in exchange for an agreement to stand behind their debt and thereby reduce the interest rates they pay. Indebted eurozone countries such as Greece could in theory leave the single currency and devalue their currencies, but, in part because there was no mechanism for a country to exit the eurozone, this would be devastating for them—which is why George Soros would argue in September 2012 that it was Germany that should "leave" if it could not "lead".[1] Deficit countries such as Greece therefore had little choice but to accept Germany's demands, which were based on its own distinctive narrative of the crisis.

Above all, Germans saw the crisis as one that had been caused by others. Even though Germany had been the first to break the terms of the SGP in 2003, they saw the crisis as one caused by the fiscal irresponsibility of other countries. They did not recognise the role that German banks had played in irresponsible lending to countries such as Greece during the boom—at the end of June 2009 Greece owed German banks €38.6 billion—let alone remember the context of reunification in which the single currency had been created.[2] In short, Germans saw themselves as victims of the crisis—a perception that was strengthened by the collective memories that had become stronger in Germany in the decade since 2000. In an article for the *Süddeutsche Zeitung* in March 2010, Joschka Fischer bemoaned the "decline in historical awareness" in Germany.[3]

Much German analysis of the crisis reflected this sense of victimhood. Oddly for a country that was thought of as "post-national", Germany tended to see the causes of the crisis in strikingly national terms. Ordinary Germans, the political establishment, and even economists seemed to look at eurozone economies in isolation from each other. They thought the crisis was caused simply by a lack of fiscal discipline in the deficit countries rather than by the interaction between eurozone countries in a poorly constructed common currency. In particular, they did not see the effect that the reformed German economy that had emerged in the 2000s had on others around it; they did not recognise that the crisis had macroeconomic causes as well as microeconomic ones and, more specifically, they did not recognise that surpluses were part of the problem of macroeconomic imbalances.

In the context of the German narrative of the crisis, Merkel's government made policy on the basis of three principles. Firstly, and above all, it sought to prevent the emergence of a "transfer union"—in other words, an EU in which fiscally responsible member states pay for fiscally irresponsible ones. Secondly, however, it also sought to prevent a break-up of the euro—not least because its exporters benefited from its weakness relative to the deutsche mark. Thirdly, it sought to maintain price stability—in other words to prevent inflation, which would have reduced the competitiveness of German exporters and reduced the value of German savings. The problem was that Germany could not have all of these things at the same time. As the crisis deepened over the next couple of years, it was forced to compromise in different ways on all three principles.

It was because of the German fear of the emergence of a "transfer union" that Merkel was initially reluctant to bail out Greece in the spring of 2010. She pointed to Article 125 of the Maastricht Treaty, which explicitly prohibited bailouts (though some said another article could be used). But to prevent an imminent Greek default in May 2010, Merkel reluctantly agreed a €750 billion rescue package and the creation of a European Financial Stability Facility, a fund to be used to help crisis countries. However, she insisted on tough conditions, including the involvement of the International Monetary Fund as part of a so-called troika with the European Commission and the European Central Bank (ECB). While Greece was required to make dramatic budget cuts and to reduce wages, Germany resisted measures to boost domestic demand. Thus the German approach was one of asymmetric adjustment: deflation in what became known as the "periphery" but no inflation in the "core".[4]

Over the next year, the Greek crisis turned into a crisis of the euro itself. The financial markets, which until the Greek crisis began had priced member states' government debt at almost identical levels, now saw the danger of a default not just in Greece but also in other eurozone countries. As Germany resisted increasing the size of the eurozone's so-called firewall, bond yields in countries such as Italy—a founder member of the EU—increased to unsustainable levels. Many economic experts began to see a mutualisation of debt in the form of so-called Eurobonds as the only possible solution. But, acutely conscious of the problem of "moral hazard", German politicians thought they had to keep pressure on deficit countries to undertake structural reform and were deliberately ambiguous about debt mutualisation, even though this kept bond yields in deficit countries such as Italy returning to unsustainably high levels. Thus Germany used bond markets as a way to enforce fiscal discipline in the eurozone.

Some saw in Chancellor Merkel's tough response to the crisis a return to classical German great power politics. *Bild*, Germany's bestselling newspaper, compared Merkel to Bismarck after she resisted the idea of a bailout in March 2010—but declared that the Germans were "Europe's fools" after she agreed to the rescue package in May. Previous chancellors worried that Merkel was departing from the principles that had guided West German foreign policy and reverting to those of a previous era. In June 2010 the former chancellor Helmut Schmidt accused the German government of "Wilhelmine pomposity" in its attitude towards France.[5] In 2011 even Helmut Kohl warned Merkel, his onetime protégée, about the danger of "throwing it all away".[6]

While the euro crisis revealed an increasingly assertive Germany within Europe, Germany was also developing closer relationships with rising powers beyond the West—what the German foreign ministry would later call *Gestaltungsmächte*, or "powers in shaping globalization".[7] In particular, the relationship between China and Germany had become even closer since the crisis began. As demand from within Europe slowed, exports to China became increasingly important to the German economy. In 2011, China accounted for just under 7 per cent of Germany's total exports, making it the third largest market for German exports, and was projected to soon overtake the US, the biggest export market outside the EU, and even France. According to one estimate, exports to China contributed 0.5 percentage points to German growth in 2011—the equivalent of €13 billion.[8]

On the back of these increasingly close economic ties, the political relationship between Berlin and Beijing was also upgraded. In June 2011 Chinese Premier Wen Jiabao came to Berlin with thirteen ministers and held a so-called government-to-government consultation—in effect, a joint cabinet meeting. Germany had previously held such meetings with other countries such as France and Israel, and also, more recently, with India. But it was the first time that China had ever established such a high-level inter-governmental negotiation mechanism with an EU member state—an extraordinary expression of Germany's importance to it. Germany was now by far the biggest European player in China.

China already seemed to have changed its approach to Europe after the rejection of the European constitution in France and the Netherlands in 2005.[9] Since then, it had focused its attention on member states rather than the EU institutions—even as the EU created a new European foreign minister and diplomatic service and tried to develop a more coherent, strategic approach to powers such as China. German diplomats sought to empower the new foreign minister to develop a "comprehensive" approach to China. But as the crisis seemed to produce a strengthened Germany, a weakened France and a marginalised UK, their Chinese counterparts responded pragmatically to German power within the EU. "If you want something done in Brussels you go to Berlin," one Chinese official said in 2012.[10]

The bilateral relationship between China and Germany was also strengthened by the way that, since the beginning of the financial crisis in 2008, the two countries had found themselves on the same side as each other—and the opposite side to the US—in debates about the global economy. This was in itself a result of shared economic interests based on the somewhat analogous roles they played in the international system. Despite the huge differences between China and Germany in terms of demography and development, there were structural similarities between their economies. Martin Wolf even created a composite of the world's two leading exporters: "Chermany".[11] Based on these structural similarities, China and Germany appeared to pursue a somewhat similar macroeconomic policy: they exerted deflationary pressure and resisted pressure to rectify economic imbalances. Thus there was what one might call a post-crisis alignment between China and Germany.

China and Germany also shared a desire to reform financial markets and global economic governance. In a joint communiqué in 2010 on their bilateral "strategic partnership", which was created under Schröder and Wen in 2004, China and Germany said that their relationship had been strengthened through the result of attempts to overcome the international financial and economic crisis.[12] They said that they shared important interests as the third and fourth largest economies in the world and as important trade and export countries, and in particular attached great value to the "real economy". Germany also promised to "actively support" China in its bid for market economy status through the EU.

The Chinese and German approach to the crisis led to disagreements between both of them and the US. As creditor countries, both were critical of the use by the US Federal Reserve of quantitative easing as a way to overcome the crisis. Conversely, at the G20 summit in Seoul in 2010, both China and Germany opposed US plans to limit current account surpluses. The Nobel Prize-winning economist Joseph Stiglitz said in an interview in 2010 that "anybody who believes China is a problem has to believe Germany is a problem."[13] (In fact, Germany would subsequently become more of a "problem" than China, whose trade surplus fell from its peak of $300 billion in 2008 to $155 billion in 2011.)

Some Chinese analysts went even further in seeing parallels between China and Germany—and by extension the potential for alignment between them. They said that, just as China was a rising global power, so Germany was a rising power within Europe. Both had in the past for different reasons been reluctant to lead or take responsibility. But the crisis increased expectations of both countries, with which they were uncomfortable, and led to criticism of both—in particular by the US—for somewhat similar reasons. Chinese analysts say that it was during this period that Wen and Merkel became closer. "We were in a similar situation," said one.[14]

Germany's excessive dependence on exports for growth, and its increasing dependence on demand from countries such as China, put it in an impossible situation. In order to correct the external imbalances within Europe, it had to become less competitive in relation to the rest of the eurozone; but the success of its export-dependent economic model depended on maintaining competitiveness as German manufacturers faced increasing competition from emerging economies outside Europe. Germany said it wanted deficit countries in Europe to become more competitive, but it did not accept that, as a corollary of this, Germany must itself become less competitive. At the same time, Germany could not abandon the euro altogether because a stronger German or even northern European currency would instantly make German exports less competitive everywhere.

Chancellor Merkel's non-committal approach to the crisis, and Germany's increasingly close relationship with powers such as China, led some analysts to wonder whether Germany might be turning away from Europe and pursuing a new *Weltpolitik*. As the German economy boomed—helped in part by capital flight from the periphery—and other eurozone economies floundered, they thought Germany might "go global alone".[15] In particular, German corporate interest in the euro area seemed to decline as big and medium-sized companies focused on high growth rates in the emerging economies.[16] But, as in the nineteenth century, Germany's geography meant it was an illusion to think it could somehow leave Europe behind. It needed Europe—if only as an export market, despite the increase in exports to emerging economies, and to keep down the value of its currency.

Thus from the summer of 2011, Merkel began to take a more proactive approach to the crisis.[17] Her advisers could not guarantee that an exit of one country such as Greece from the euro would not lead to contagion or even a break-up—which would be devastating for Germany. She therefore resolved to keep Greece in, even though this would involve more fiscal transfers and increase Germany's liability for European debt. But, while calling for "more Europe", Merkel continued to resist committing to a more open-ended debt mutualisation in the form of Eurobonds. In September 2011, the Constitutional Court approved the bailout of Greece and the creation of the European Financial Stability Facility (EFSF), but ruled that open-ended debt mutualisation would violate the Basic Law. In other words, Germany could go no further in terms of debt mutualisation without amending its constitution.

Instead, Germany focused on reducing government debt and improving "competitiveness" in Europe. In countries such as Ireland and Spain, the problem, at least until the crisis began, had been excessive private rather than public debt. But Germans continued to look at it through the prism of Greece—what Paul Krugman called the "Hellenization" of discourse about the euro crisis.[18] Thus in 2011 it pushed through a series of measures designed to solve what Germans saw above all as a *Schuldenkrise*, or debt crisis—that is, one caused by fiscal irresponsibility. As part of the so-called Six-Pack, it introduced a new Macroeconomic Imbalance Procedure, which was tougher on deficits than surpluses. The fiscal compact, which was agreed at the European Council in December 2011, required all eurozone countries to enact an equivalent of the constitutional amendment passed by Germany in 2009 that required it to maintain a balanced budget.

The effects of this coordinated and prolonged austerity within the eurozone was to increase the pain in countries such as Greece, whose economy was 20 per cent smaller by the end of 2012 than in 2007. But it did not solve the problem of bond spreads, which many economists saw as fundamental. They argued that a "feedback loop" between bad banks and sovereign debt made insolvency a self-fulfilling prophecy. The ECB had taken some measures to break the link—in particular, after taking over as ECB president at end of 2011, Mario Draghi introduced a new bond buying programme, the so-called Long-Term Refinancing Operations (LTRO). But by the summer of 2012, while German bond yields had fallen to record lows, Italian and Spanish bond yields were once again at unsustainable levels. A few days before the European Council in June 2012, Merkel declared that there would be no Eurobonds in her lifetime.

At the European Council a few days later, the new French president François Hollande, the new Italian prime minister Mario Monti and the Spanish prime minister Mariano Rajoy joined forces to overrule Germany. They agreed to enable the European Stability Mechanism (ESM), the permanent successor to the EFSF, to recapitalise banks in crisis countries directly. While in much of Europe it was seen as a breakthrough that finally broke the "feedback loop" between bad banks and sovereign debt, in Germany it was seen as a defeat—*Spiegel* called it "the night Merkel lost".[19] In London the following month, Draghi promised to do "whatever it takes" to preserve the euro. Shortly afterwards, he announced a programme of unlimited bond purchases on the secondary market to help bring down bond spreads within the eurozone—so-called

Outright Monetary Transactions (OMT). Many Germans such as Bundesbank President Jens Weidmann, the only member of the ECB's twenty-three-member Governing Council who voted against OMT, now saw a creeping mutualisation of European debt—the "transfer union" that Germany had tried from the beginning of the crisis to prevent.

Many Germans also feared that the measures taken by Draghi were inflationary—though most Anglo-Saxon economists thought deflation was a greater danger than inflation. In a cover story in August 2012, *Spiegel* warned that the eurozone's inflationary monetary policy amounted to a creeping "Enteignung", or "expropriation", of German savings—a term that invoked the Nazi theft of Jewish property during the Third Reich.[20] In an extraordinary speech in Frankfurt in September 2012, Weidmann even implicitly compared Draghi to the devil. Speaking on the 180th anniversary of Goethe's death, he reminded listeners of the "money creation" scene in Act One of the second part of *Faust*, in which Mephistopheles persuades the emperor to print money—with disastrous consequences. He said Goethe had correctly identified "the core problem of today's paper money-based monetary policy" and the "potentially dangerous correlation of paper money creation, state financing and inflation".[21]

Although many thought the eurozone had not yet gone far enough in integrating, the crisis had by the end of 2012 produced "more Europe", as Merkel and other pro-Europeans had called for.[22] The crisis had been the catalyst for a process of accelerated integration in which member states transferred powers to the European level, particularly (but not only) over their economies, which would have been unthinkable under other circumstances. In the summer of 2012, European Council President Herman van Rompuy outlined a series of "building blocks" towards a "genuine economic and monetary union", including a banking union, fiscal union, and even political union.[23] In a lecture in Oxford in October 2012, German Finance Minister Wolfgang Schäuble—seen as the most "pro-European" member of Merkel's cabinet—said that "far from undoing the European project, the crisis has been helping to advance it."[24]

However, the steps taken since the crisis differed in important ways from those taken in previous phases of European integration. The integration that had begun with the Schuman Plan in 1950 was based on voluntary rather than forced transfer of sovereignty. But what had happened since the crisis began was something between voluntary and forced transfer of sovereignty. Technically, member states had agreed to transfer sovereignty to the European level in the same ways as in the past; no one was forced to agree to further integration. In reality, nonetheless, eurozone countries had little choice but to transfer powers to the EU level: as European leaders such as Merkel themselves repeatedly told them, there was no alternative. In that sense, it was what might be called "integration at gunpoint".

In order to fix flaws in the architecture of monetary union, the EU, led by Germany, also introduced a much stricter system of rules and enforcement of rules. The crisis had dramatically revealed the failure of the Maastricht regime, which had been reformed in 2005 after France and Germany had in effect suspended the Stability and Growth Pact, to produce economic convergence in the single-currency area. Nevertheless, the eurozone countries, led by Germany, sought to extend and tighten the system of rules created by Maastricht, as well as strengthen their enforcement.[25] The "Maastricht III" system that emerged from the crisis, based on the series of measures taken since the crisis that culminated in the fiscal compact, was more intrusive and imposed stricter conditionality and greater homogeneity in the EU than its two predecessors.

Thus what seemed to be emerging from the crisis was a more coercive EU—in other words, one in which coercion plays a greater role than in the past. This in turn created tensions between member states (that is, between surplus countries and deficit countries) and within member states (that is, between elites and citizens). In particular, the troika—the ad hoc grouping of the European Central Bank, European Commission and International Monetary Fund that enforced austerity in crisis countries such as Greece—was seen as a kind of occupying force. This more coercive EU seemed a world away from the vision of its founding fathers. The morning after the fiscal compact was agreed upon at the European summit in December 2011, Ian Traynor wrote in the *Guardian* that what was emerging from the euro crisis was "a joyless union of penalties, punishments, disciplines and seething resentments".[26]

As well as becoming more coercive, Europe was also becoming more German. As Germany gradually took on more liability for European debt, it also sought more control. Thus although many were relieved by Germany's apparent commitment to the euro and the EU, the new approach in some ways exacerbated fears about German power. Germany used its unprecedented power to impose its economic preferences, based on the lessons it had drawn from its own history, on the eurozone. In short, Germany sought to universalise its history and remake Europe in its own image. The consequence of this approach was that the stricter conditionality being imposed was perceived in deficit countries such as Greece and Italy as imposed by Berlin rather than Brussels: the occupying force was seen as a German one. This unprecedented identification of the EU with one member state made conditionality harder to impose and increased resistance to it—and led to the surge of collective memories from World War II.

Some even saw in Germany's approach a kind of economic imperialism. In particular, critics of Germany pointed to the asymmetric adjustment process on which it had insisted since the beginning of the crisis—deflation in the periphery without inflation in Germany. "This is not a monetary union," Martin Wolf wrote in May 2012. "It is far more like an empire."[27] George Soros pointed out that debate about the crisis had taken place using the terminology of centre and periphery—terms that are normally used to describe imperial relationships rather than geography. He warned of the danger of the emergence of a Europe permanently divided between surplus and deficit countries—"a German empire with the periphery as the hinterland".[28] The danger, in other words, was not so much that Germany would desert Europe but, as in the past, that it would dominate it.

For a brief moment, however, it seemed as if Germany might be prepared, in a kind of equivalent of the moment in 1790 when US Treasury Secretary Alexander Hamilton agreed to assume liability for state debts, to strike a grand bargain with the rest of Europe: full debt liability for political union. In the second half of 2012, there was much discussion of political union, which would require a major change to the European Treaties and a referendum under Article 146 of the German constitution—the article Jürgen Habermas had wanted to invoke in 1990.[29] But such an approach was fraught with difficulty: it was not just unclear whether other eurozone countries such as France would agree to political union, which had yet to be defined, it was also unclear whether Germans would vote for it. By the beginning of 2013, Germany had turned away from political union and even hollowed out banking union—not least because OMT had made the crisis less acute and relieved the pressure on Germany. The problem of German power in Europe thus remained unresolved.

* * *

However, while Germany's response to the crisis led to an increasing perception of dominance in Europe, it continued to resist pressure to devote resources to solving international crises and in particular to make a contribution to European security commensurate with its size. Its defence budget remained relatively low at 1.3 per cent of GDP. To some extent, this was part of a Europe-wide trend: US Secretary of Defense Robert Gates, for example, spoke in 2010 of the "demilitarization of Europe".[30] Nevertheless, although other European countries such as France and the UK were cutting their defence budgets as they sought fiscal consolidation in response to the crisis—in France's case, under German pressure—they continued to spend significantly more as a proportion of GDP than Germany and still aimed to project power in the world. There was a danger not just of a "two-tiered" NATO, as Gates feared, but of a "two-tiered" EU divided between security providers and consumers.[31]

The most dramatic illustration of Germany's reluctance to contribute to security, even in a multilateral context, was Berlin's abstention in the UN Security Council vote in March 2011 on military intervention to prevent a massacre of Libyan pro-democracy protesters by Muammar Gaddafi's forces in Benghazi. In abstaining, Germany broke not just with the US but also with France—in that sense, it was an even more dramatic break with Germany's meta-level preferences than over Iraq in 2003. Germany also withdrew seventy German personnel operating AWACS planes in the Mediterranean as part of a NATO mission. There was a striking contrast between Germany's approach to this crisis and its approach to the military intervention in Kosovo twelve years earlier, not just because this time it refused to participate in, or even support, the military intervention, but also because the Holocaust—which was used to justify German involvement in Operation Allied Force in 1999—was entirely absent from the discussion.

Just weeks later, it emerged that the German government had secretly agreed a €1.5 billion deal to sell 200 Leopard 2 tanks to Saudi Arabia—which had sent troops to Bahrain to help the authorities there put down pro-democracy protests in March.[32] The conjuncture of the Libya abstention and the Saudi deal neatly illustrated the tension in German foreign policy in response to the Arab revolutions. But the sale of tanks to Saudi Arabia was actually part of a much bigger boom in German arms exports. Germany approved the sale of about €1.2 billion in arms to the United Arab Emirates and various weapons systems including frigates and Fuchs armoured personnel carriers to Algeria. It was what *Spiegel* later called the "Merkel doctrine": do not intervene but sell weapons.[33] Officials said the aim was, above all, to secure the capacity of the German defence industry at a time when Western powers were cutting budgets.

Arms exports had always been a kind of blind spot in the Federal Republic's "civilian power" identity. Although the Federal Republic had rejected the use of military force as a foreign-policy tool, it had, unlike Japan, continued to sell weapons. In 2000, Germany issued new guidelines restricting arms sales, but they did not stop arms manufacturers booming along with the rest of Germany's exporters in the 2000s. Between 2006 and 2010, Germany was the third largest exporter of major conventional weapons after the United States and Russia, with 11 per cent of the global market compared to 7 per cent for France and 4 per cent for the UK.[34] In 2011, German arms export permits reached €5 billion for the first time—and 42 per cent of them went to non-NATO countries.[35] In other words, just as other German manufacturers were becoming increasingly reliant on emerging economies—many of them undemocratic—so were German arms manufacturers.

Thus there was a striking contrast between German foreign policy within Europe and beyond Europe. While Germany was increasingly assertive within Europe, it was strangely unassertive throughout the rest of the world, reluctant to play a role commensurate with its economic power. German diplomats pointed to the failures of Western military intervention in Iraq and elsewhere and said their non-confrontational approach was better. They thought of rising powers as *Gestaltungsmächte*, or "powers in shaping globalisation", with whom one could develop "strategic partnerships" as a bilateral way of improving global governance—in other words, a step towards multilateralism, rather than an alternative to it. Above all, Germany could promote the model of regional integration the EU represented. Meanwhile, of course, it could also promote exports of cars and machines—including weapons.

There was a certain logic to the idea of pursuing one foreign policy within Europe and another beyond it. In an influential pamphlet for the British think tank Demos that was published in 1999, the British diplomat Robert Cooper distinguished between a Westphalian "modern world" of classic nation states, the balance of power and military force, and a post-Westphalian "post-modern world" in which the distinction between domestic and foreign affairs was blurred, collective security had replaced the balance of power, and military force was no longer a legitimate tool.[36] While EU member states were "post-modern states living on a post-modern continent", much of the rest of the world remained "modern". Europeans therefore needed to "get used to the idea of double standards".[37] Europeans could operate on the basis of laws and cooperative security with each other, but when dealing with "modern" states, they needed to revert to "the rougher methods of an earlier era"—in particular, military force where necessary.[38]

Oddly, however, German foreign policy seemed to be almost the diametric opposite of the one suggested by Cooper. Of course, no EU member state could use or even threaten to use military force within Europe, and Germany was more reluctant than France or the UK to use it beyond Europe. But, as the crisis had shown, Germany was prepared to use economic power—another form of hard power—assertively as a way to coerce other states in Europe, where, before 1945, it had always expanded.[39] Beyond Europe, on the other hand, it tended to reject not just the use of military force, but even the use of economic power as a means of achieving strategic objectives, and seemed to think it could depend on soft power alone—almost as if the rest of the world were nothing but an export market.

Germany could no longer be described as a "civilian power". Before reunification and even in the first decade after it, the Federal Republic had, alongside Japan, come closer than any other state to the ideal-typical foreign-policy role described by Hanns Maull. But in the 2000s German multilateralism had weakened and Germany had pursued a realist foreign policy based on the pursuit of economic objectives. The comparisons with Bismarck that some made after the Greek crisis began suggested that Germany was once again an old-fashioned great power. And yet Germany hardly seemed to be reverting to the bellicose, expansionist foreign policy of the nineteenth century. In fact, part of the reason for the perception gap between Germany and the rest of Europe was that Germans felt that, by rejecting the use of military force, they had made a decisive break with the past.

Thus Germany is once again a paradox. It is both powerful and weak—in fact, as in the late nineteenth century after unification, it seems powerful from the outside but feels vulnerable to many Germans. It does not want to "lead" and resists debt mutualisation, but at the same time seeks to remake Europe in its own image in order to make it more "competitive". German power is characterised by a strange mixture of economic assertiveness and military abstinence. Germany is increasingly using its economic power within Europe to impose its preferences on other member states—and in that sense is "normal". But it has few of the ambitions of France and the UK to project power beyond Europe, where it seeks above all to sell more cars and machines, and in particular rejects the use of military force—in that sense it is "abnormal".

One way of understanding the paradox of German power is through Edward Luttwak's concept of "geo-economics".[40] In an essay in *The National Interest* in 1990—almost exactly the same time that Maull was applying the concept of a "civilian power" to Germany—Luttwak argued that "methods of commerce" were "displacing military methods" in international relations—"with disposable capital in lieu of firepower, civilian innovation in lieu of military-technical advancement, and market penetration in lieu of garrisons and bases".[41] Luttwak argued that, although states were increasingly using one kind of tool rather than another, international relations would continue to follow the "logic of conflict", which was "adversarial, zero-sum, and paradoxical".[42] The term "geo-economics" was meant to capture this "admixture of the logic of conflict with the methods of commerce—or, as Clausewitz would have written, the logic of war in the grammar of commerce".[43]

The events of the next two decades seemed to disprove Luttwak's thesis of a shift from geopolitics to "geo-economics". The regional and ethnic conflicts of the 1990s and then 9/11 forced Western states to use military power. As we have seen, even states such as Germany that had for various reasons been reluctant to use military force came under increasing pressure to contribute to conflict resolution not just financially but also in terms of troops on the ground. In fact, in the first decade of the post-Cold War world, it seemed as if conventional military power was more rather than less important than it had been previously. However, subsequent developments—in particular the shift in the global distribution of power away from the US towards rising powers such as China—seem to have vindicated Luttwak's argument.

In particular, the concept of "geo-economics" now seems particularly helpful as a way of describing how Germany has become more assertive in its use of economic power within the EU. Beyond Europe, Germany is a geo-economic power in the "soft" sense that it seems to focus almost exclusively on the pursuit of economic objectives. But within the eurozone, as a zero-sum competition between the "core" and the "periphery" seems to have replaced what seemed to be a win-win situation, Germany has also used its economic power to coerce other states through tough conditionality. Thus Germany may be a geo-economic power within Europe in the "hard", or Luttwakian, sense that it uses economic means in a way that seems more Clausewitzian than Kantian.

According to Luttwak, the nature of a "geo-economic power" is determined by the role that the state plays in the economy. As he acknowledges, "while states occupy virtually all of the world's political space, they occupy only a fraction of the total economic space."[44] He suggests that forms of coexistence between "geo-economically active" states and private economic actors will vary: in some cases, it is intense and in others it is distant; in some cases states "guide" large companies for their own geo-economic purposes and in others companies seek to manipulate politicians or bureaucracies. The relationship between the German state and business seems to be an example of what Luttwak calls "reciprocal manipulation".[45] German companies demand that the German state make policy that promotes their interests; they in turn help politicians maximise growth and in particular employment levels—the key measure of success in German politics.

This coexistence is particularly intense between the state—particularly the economics ministry—and exporters. The disproportionate contribution of exports to growth means that German politicians are extremely dependent on exporters. However, because much of this growth has come from exports to economies such as China and Russia in which the state dominates business, exporters are also conversely dependent on the German government. As exports have increased as a share of GDP in the last decade, especially since the Schröder government, German exporters seem to have exerted greater influence on German foreign policy.

Of course, Germany is not the only "geo-economically active" state in the world. Other states, for example China, also use economic means for strategic objectives. However, China apparently aspires to be a straightforward great power: although it relies primarily on economic power at this moment in its rise, it is also committed to the use of military power—what Luttwak called a "superior modality". An influential concept among Chinese foreign-policy analysts is that of "comprehensive national power"—the idea that a successful foreign policy must be based on a "balanced power-profile" that includes military, political and economic power.[46] In that sense, Chinese foreign policy can be seen as a kind of neo-mercantilism. Germany, on the other hand, is unique in its combination of economic assertiveness and military abstinence. In a sense, therefore, it may be the purest example of a "geo-economic power" in the world today.

CONCLUSION

GEO-ECONOMIC SEMI-HEGEMONY

From 1871 until 1945, as we have seen, Germany created instability in Europe. Its size and central location—the so-called *Mittellage*—made it too powerful for a balance of power but not powerful enough to exercise hegemony. The German question appeared to have been resolved after World War II by the division of Germany and by the integration of the Federal Republic into the West through NATO and the EU. With the transformation of Europe since the end of the Cold War, Germany returned to the *Mittellage* in a geographic sense. But whereas in the past Germany faced potential enemies on all sides and feared encirclement, it is now surrounded on all sides by NATO allies and EU partners. Germany's post-reunification "strategic saturation" and the interdependence of its economy with that of its neighbours means that it no longer seeks territorial expansion and no longer feels threatened. In other words, in geopolitical terms, Germany is benign.

However, the size of Germany's economy, and the interdependence between it and those around it, is now creating instability within Europe in an analogous way. After reunification, Germany became bigger but was initially economically weaker as it struggled to deal with the costs of assimilating East Germany. Moreover, it saw its interests as being aligned with its NATO allies and EU partners. But during the last decade, as the German economy has recovered, Germany has become more willing to impose its preferences on others. Within the context of the EU, Germany's economy is too big for any of its neighbours, such as France, to challenge—a "colossus", as Jürgen Habermas called it in 2010.[1] In short, what appears to have happened is that the "German question" has re-emerged in geo-economic form.

Against the background of the euro crisis, there has been much discussion of the emergence of German "hegemony" in Europe.[2] Since the crisis began, policymakers and journalists have routinely described Germany as Europe's hegemon. Some have qualified the description by describing Germany as a "Hegemon wider willen" or a "reluctant hegemon"—in other words a power in denial about its proper role—and have called on it to be bolder.[3] In a speech in Berlin in November 2011, for example, Polish Foreign Minister Radek Sikorski said he feared German power less than he was beginning to fear Germany inactivity, and urged Germany to lead Europe.[4] But the reason Germany does not qualify as a hegemon is not so much its shyness, as its self-centeredness and short-termism. Nor is it even a potential hegemon. As in the past, it is too small to take on the burdens of hegemony.

The debate about German "hegemony" in Europe since the crisis has been strangely disconnected from the history of the German question discussed in Chapter 1 of this book. Rather, the calls for German leadership have been based on so-called hegemonic stability theory, according to which a hegemon sets norms but also creates a system of incentives for those further down the order to benefit and therefore stay in the system. In particular, it makes short-term concessions to those co-opted in the hegemonic hierarchy in order to serve its own long-term interests. One of the paradigmatic examples of hegemony of this kind is the United States after the end of World War II, which in the 1950s allowed western Europeans to trade preferentially—and in the process discriminate against American imports—in pursuit of its strategic interest in European stability. Thus the US made enlightened use of power.

For hegemonic stability theorists, the alternative to hegemony in international relations is instability. In *The World in Depression, 1929–1939*, Charles Kindleberger argued that a global economy runs smoothly only in the presence of a hegemon that underwrites stability. In the 1930s, after the Wall Street Crash, the absence of a hegemon had caused a breakdown of the international system. In particular, Kindleberger criticised the US for its reluctance to take over leadership of the global economy from Britain—at a time when Germany was in a similar position as the deficit countries now. As a State Department official in the late 1940s, Kindleberger was one of the architects of the Marshall Plan—an attempt to avoid the mistake he believed the US had made during the Great Depression.

Hegemonic stability theory informed the thinking of some German policymakers. In particular, Wolfgang Schäuble referred to Kindleberger and said he believed that his insights should be applied to the euro crisis. In a speech at the height of the crisis, he said that "Kindleberger's central message is more important in 2010 than ever before." That was, he said, that only "a leading nation, a benign hegemon or 'stabilizer'" could create and maintain a stable global economy.[5] The lesson, he went on, was that Germany and France must in effect become the hegemon that Europe needed. But instead of making enlightened use of power like the US after 1945, since the crisis began Germany seems to have simply imposed its own preferences on others in the eurozone, in so far as it has been able to, and to have pursued short-term rather than long-term interests.

Given Germany's clear interest in the survival of the euro—not least because its weakness compared to the deutsche mark benefits German exports—the equivalent of the US role towards Europe after 1945 might have been for Germany to take measures to reduce its trade surplus, to allow a moderate increase in inflation, or to act as a consumer of last resort in order to help indebted economies grow their way out of recession and thus reduce their debt. However, Germany has consistently refused to take such an approach. Instead, it has insisted on austerity throughout the eurozone, which has made it harder for the periphery to grow its way out of recession and exacerbated the crisis. While unemployment in Germany is now at its lowest level since reunification, it has reached record levels in other countries such as Spain. There has been no Marshall Plan for the indebted economies of Europe.

In fact, in some ways, Germany has not created stability—the central role, according to hegemonic stability theory, of a hegemon—but *instability* in Europe. Germany's rhetoric focuses on stability: it talks about a "stability union" and is proud of its *Stabilitätskultur*, or "stability culture". But its definition of the concept is extremely narrow: when Germany talks about stability it means price stability and nothing else. In fact, in attempting to export its "stability culture", Germany has in a broader sense created instability. In particular, its ongoing reticence about the extent to which it will accept mutualisation of European debt—apparently a deliberate strategy in order to maintain pressure on indebted countries to reform—has created a climate of uncertainty. Thus one might almost speak of a German "instability culture".

Since the euro crisis began, Germany has exported rules but not norms. Many in other eurozone countries see the rules as serving Germany's national interest rather than their own. Thus they have often submitted only reluctantly to German demands. They have sought to resist, to drag their feet and to backtrack on commitments they have made. In other words, there has been no hegemonic consent—one of the features of hegemony that distinguishes it from empire. There is no "Berlin Consensus" analogous to the "Washington Consensus". In some ways, Germany is now even less of a hegemon than the Bonn Republic was. As a "cooperative hegemon" together with France before German reunification and EU enlargement, it successfully "uploaded" its own preferences with the consent of its European partners.[6]

This failure by Germany to play the role of a European hegemon that some, such as Sikorski, want it to reflects the limits of its geo-economic power. Germany's economy had recovered in the 2000s, but largely, as we have seen, through wage restraint and a favourable environment. It remains too fragile to take on the burdens of hegemony, whether through fiscal transfers or a mutualisation of European debt or moderate inflation. In fact, as we have seen, Germany pursues the economic policy of a small country rather than Europe's biggest economy. In short, although Germany's increased power and France's relative weakness has allowed Germany to impose its preferences on others in the eurozone, it is too small to be a European hegemon. This is strikingly similar to the position of Germany within Europe between 1871 and 1945. In other words, Germany seems to have returned to the position of semi-hegemony that Ludwig Dehio described—except in geo-economic form.[7]

In this sense, the Europe that is emerging from the crisis is not so much German as chaotic. In particular, what German geo-economic semi-hegemony is likely to mean is more conflict in Europe. Economists have argued that Germany's approach to the euro crisis is exacerbating tensions between European countries. By insisting on running a persistent surplus, for example, Germany is putting impossible pressure on its European partners—not so much an optimum currency area as "an area built around a core country which structurally absorbs liquidity", as Lucio Caracciolo puts it.[8] But aside from this economic logic, the history of international relations in Europe—and in particular the history of the German question discussed in Chapter 1—tells us that German semi-hegemony is likely to produce conflict in some form. The danger in Europe now is of a geo-economic version of the conflicts within Europe that followed unification in 1871.

What this may mean is a return to the competitive dynamic of coalition formation among great powers in Europe before 1945. Some have argued that, since the crisis began, Europe has reverted to a system in which relations between states are based on power rather than the rule of law. But in the institutionalised yet dynamic context of the EU, power is often a matter of the ability to define rules—particularly on economic policy. In order to "upload" their preferences to the EU level, member states form coalitions. Initially, the Franco-German couple was the most important bilateral relationship in the EU. After enlargement, coalition building became more difficult and a complex network structure developed within the EU. But since the start of the crisis the dynamic of coalition building has centred on Germany as member states have adopted a mixture of bandwagoning and counterbalancing in relation to it.

Much bilateral diplomacy within the EU since the crisis began has centred on Berlin. Most member states have tried to develop closer relationships with Germany, which is increasingly seen as the decisive player on economic and other issues. Berlin is once again the "diplomatic capital of Europe", as it was in the 1880s. In fact, a kind of hub-and-spoke relational structure may be replacing the network structure that has existed within the EU since enlargement. In particular, the countries of central Europe whose economies have been integrated with Germany's since reunification are beginning to form a kind of geo-economic equivalent of a sphere of influence. Countries such as Poland that felt threatened by Russia see in German investment a kind of security guarantee. Some analysts have even perceived the re-emergence of a German-dominated *Mitteleuropa*.[9]

At the same time, however, other EU member states—in particular those of the so-called periphery—have found themselves under increased pressure to form what George Soros has called a "common front" against Germany.[10] After unification in 1871, no other European power was powerful enough to stand against Germany on its own and they therefore had little choice but to form an anti-German coalition to balance it. This in turn created the *cauchemar des coalitions* in Germany. At the end of the nineteenth century what Hans-Peter Schwarz called the "dialectic of encirclement" produced such a coalition and ultimately led to World War I. Now Germany fears being encircled by weak economies rather than potential military rivals. Though the means are different, German power is once again such that other European countries have little choice but to join forces—the geo-economic equivalent of encirclement.

There are already signs of a German fear of this type of geo-economic encirclement within the eurozone.[11] In particular, Germans fear a takeover of the ECB, which, instead of exporting the *Stabilitätskultur* of the Bundesbank to the rest of Europe as they had hoped, is now perceived to be importing others' weak currency culture into Germany. These fears have increased since the June 2012 European summit, which was seen as a breakthrough in much of Europe but as a defeat in Germany. Some German economists now think the ECB is shifting from a hawkish German model to an inflationary Latin model, and even that France, Italy and Spain—the three countries that joined forces in June 2012—are the new eurozone "core". In short, they fear that power is shifting to the debtors. This perception is strengthened by the sense of German victimhood that, as we have seen, has emerged since the Millennium—strikingly illustrated by the use of terms such as "Enteignung", or "expropriation".

Thus a new geo-economic version of the "dialectic of encirclement" has emerged within Europe. In other words, the geopolitical dilemmas that Europe struggled with for centuries have returned in geo-economic form. In particular, they centre on a conflict between the interests of creditor and debtor countries locked into a single-currency area. In debt crises, creditor countries tend to be a minority, but whereas they coordinate effectively, debtor countries face greater problems of collective action because they have an interest in differentiating themselves from each other.[12] In this case, much will depend on the approach of France, which has so far baulked at the idea of forming, and presumably leading, an anti-German coalition. The question is how much conflict will be needed within Europe to resolve this dynamic.

In a sense, therefore, history has returned to Europe. Despite the transformation of Germany since 1945, there are striking parallels between its ideological development after unification in 1871 and since reunification in 1990—in particular the idea of a German mission. But perhaps even more importantly, there are structural parallels between then and now. In particular, we seem to be back to a competitive Europe centred on a powerful Germany, which has reverted to something like its pre-1945 position of "semi-hegemony". However, the transformation of Europe through the EU and the euro means we are not back to the "the world of 1913", as President Mitterrand feared in 1989: there is no question of war. But the re-emergence of the German question in geo-economic form means that, although the means are different, the dynamic is analogous.

This book began with Heinrich August Winkler's idea of Germany's "long road west". A big part of this story was the belated development of political freedom in Germany. Winkler writes that, in so far as it makes sense to speak of a German *Sonderweg*, it is above all because of its later and more problematic development of democratic values.[13] Germany is not becoming less democratic—though there is within Germany much debate about a "crisis" in democracy. Since 1945, it has gradually developed a Western political culture that has proven more vibrant and resilient than some expected. In the 1960s, some worried that, although West Germans had supported democracy during the *Wirtschaftswunder*, the Federal Republic could not cope with a recession, but these fears were not realised. In that sense, Germany has, at least internally, overcome its aberration from what Winkler calls the "normative project of the West".[14]

There is, however, a question about whether Germany will remain part of the West in strategic terms. Since reunification, a shift in German foreign policy has taken place against the background of a changed strategic environment after the end of the Cold War. In particular, the relationship with the US has changed and is not likely to revert to the Cold War paradigm—a codependent but unequal relationship. There is also increasingly a tendency in Germany to pursue a "German way"—a key element of German nationalism. The new German nationalism may centre on peace and exports. But there is nevertheless a tendency in Germany to separate itself from—and see itself as superior to—the West. In particular, since Iraq and the economic crisis, there is a new scepticism in Germany about, and even contempt for, Anglo-Saxon ideas—strengthened by the recent revelations of spying on Germans, including Chancellor Merkel herself, by American and British intelligence agencies.

The *Westbindung* as a security arrangement preceded the Federal Republic's development of a liberal political culture. For forty years, it was an existential necessity that overrode other foreign-policy objectives. However, over the last twenty years—in other words, just as Germany completed its "long road west"—that imperative has gradually disappeared. Now, for the first time, the *Westbindung* is a choice. The foreign-policy parameters of the Federal Republic—the meta-level preferences that go back to Adenauer—are being increasingly questioned. Although it is hard to see how Germany could abandon Europe, it is quite possible to imagine a post-Western German foreign policy. According to one poll in 2011, Germans were split three ways about whether they should continue to co-operate primarily with their partners in the West, with other countries such as China, India and Russia, or both.[15]

Shortly after Angela Merkel was elected to a third term as chancellor in September 2013—this time in a grand coalition with the Social Democrats—the renewed debate about Germany's relationship with the West dramatically intensified. After Ukrainian President Viktor Yanukovych rejected an Association Agreement with the EU and pro-European protesters occupied the Maidan in Kiev, Russia invaded and annexed Crimea. For the first time since the end of the Cold War, borders in Europe once again seemed vulnerable. Merkel insisted on the need for a political solution to the crisis, but after Russia further destabilised eastern Ukraine, she agreed to impose tough EU sanctions on Russia, despite the impact on German exporters and Germany's dependence on Russian gas. Thus Germany seemed to some extent to re-prioritise strategic objectives over economic ones—at least in relation to Russia.

However, the Ukraine crisis also led to a revival of the idea of "equidistance" between Russia and the West. While much of the German political establishment seemed to experience a kind of "geopolitical awakening", many ordinary Germans were deeply resistant to the idea of confronting Russia. One poll in early April 2014 showed 49 per cent supporting the idea that Germany should mediate between Russia and the West, compared to only 45 percent who wanted Germany to side with its EU partners and NATO allies.[16] In eastern Germany, 60 per cent wanted Germany to mediate and only 31 per cent wanted it to side with the West. The poll led one commentator to speak of a "schleichende Entwestlichung", or "creeping de-Westernisation" of Germany and Winkler himself said there was "cause to doubt" whether Germany remained committed to the West.[17] German history, in other words, is not yet at an end.

NOTES

INTRODUCTION: THE RETURN OF HISTORY?

1. Heinrich August Winkler, *Germany: The Long Road West. Volume II: 1933–1990* (Oxford: Oxford University Press, 2007), p. 571.
2. Ibid., p. 580.
3. Heinrich August Winkler, "Greatness and Limits of the West. The History of an Unfinished Project", Ralf Dahrendorf Lecture, London School of Economics, 7 October 2010, available at http://www.lse.ac.uk/europeanInstitute/LEQS/LEQSPaper30.pdf
4. Ibid., p. 571.
5. Andrew Moravcsik, "Europe after the Crisis", *Foreign Affairs*, May/June 2012, available at http://www.foreignaffairs.com/articles/137421/andrew-moravcsik/europe-after-the-crisis
6. See for example Tony Barber, "Greeks direct cries of pain at Germany", *Financial Times*, 14 February 2012, available at http://www.ft.com/intl/cms/s/0/67ff90dc-5728-11e1-869b-00144feabdc0.html#axzz1p4kMceBT
7. Richard Clogg, "In Athens", *London Review of Books*, 5 July 2012, available at http://www.lrb.co.uk/v34/n13/richard-clogg/in-athens
8. Rachel Donadio/Nicholas Kulish, "Official Warmth and Public Rage for Merkel in Athens", *New York Times*, 9 October 2012, available at http://www.nytimes.com/2012/10/10/world/europe/angela-merkel-greece-visit.html?_r=0
9. "Jean-Claude Juncker Interview: 'The Demons Haven't Been Banished'", Spiegel Online, 11 March 2013, available at http://www.spiegel.de/international/europe/spiegel-interview-with-luxembourg-prime-minister-juncker-a-888021.html
10. "L'Elysée s'abstient de critiquer Angela Merkel pour ne pas apparaître laxiste auprès des marchés", *Le Monde*, 19 March 2010, available at http://www.lemonde.fr/europe/

article/2010/03/19/l-elysee-s-abstient-de-critiquer-angela-merkel-pour-ne-pas-apparaitre-laxiste-aupres-des-marches_1321300_3214.html

11. Author interview with Hans-Ulrich Klose, Berlin, 26 April 2010.

1. THE GERMAN QUESTION

1. Brendan Simms, *Europe: The Struggle for Supremacy, 1453 to the Present* (London: Allen Lane, 2013), p. 243.
2. Speech on 9 February 1871, available at http://germanhistorydocs.ghi-dc.org/sub_document.cfm?document_id=1849. See also Jonathan Steinberg, *Bismarck: A Life* (Oxford: Oxford University Press, 2011), p. 312–13.
3. In international relations theory, great powers are generally defined in terms of their relative military capabilities. For example John Mearsheimer writes that "to qualify as a great power, a state must have sufficient military assets to put up a serious fight in an all-out conventional war against the most powerful state in the world. The candidate need not have the capability to defeat the leading state, but it must have some reasonable prospect of turning the conflict into a war of attrition that leaves the dominant state seriously weakened, even if that dominant state ultimately wins the war." John Mearsheimer, *The Tragedy of Great Power Politics* (New York: Norton, 2002), p. 5.
4. Imanuel Geiss, *The Question of German reunification, 1806–1996* (London: Routledge, 1997).
5. See Gordon A. Craig, *Germany, 1866–1945* (Oxford: Oxford University Press, 1978) p. 15.
6. Population figures from A.J.P. Taylor, *The Struggle for Mastery in Europe, 1848–1918* (Oxford: Oxford University Press, 1971), p. xxv.
7. See Steinberg, *Bismarck*, p. 313.
8. Ludwig Dehio, *Germany and World Politics in the Twentieth Century* (New York: Norton, 1959), p. 15. Originally published as *Deutschland und die Weltpolitik im 20. Jahrhundert* (Munich: Verlag R. Oldenbourg, 1955). The term Dehio uses in German is "Halbhegemonie", which is translated as "semi-supremacy". However, I prefer the term "semi-hegemony", which maintains the link to the concept of "hegemony".
9. Hans-Peter Schwarz, *Die Zentralmacht Europas: Deutschlands Rückkehr auf die Weltbühne* (Berlin: Siedler Verlag, 1994), p. 204.
10. Henry Kissinger, *Diplomacy* (New York: Simon and Schuster, 1994), p. 134.
11. Bismarck originally used the phrase in 1876 and referred to a Pomeranian "musketeer". In a speech in 1888 he replaced "musketeer" with "grenadier", which became the more famous version. See A.J.P. Taylor, *Bismarck: The Man and the Statesman* (Harmondsworth: Penguin, 1995), p. 167.
12. Craig, *Germany, 1866–1945*, p. 115.

13. Ibid., p. 116.
14. Ibid., p. 102.
15. Simms, *Europe: The Struggle for Supremacy*, p. 239.
16. A.J.P. Taylor, *The Course of German History* (London: Hamish Hamilton, 1945), p. 68.
17. Michael Hughes, *Nationalism and Society: Germany, 1800–1945* (London: Edward Arnold, 1988), p. 22.
18. Craig, *Germany, 1866–1945*, p. 36.
19. I would like to thank Karen Leeder for her help in translating these lines.
20. On this "empire talk" from the 1880s onwards, see Geoff Eley, "Imperial imaginary, colonial effect: writing the colony and the metropole together", in Catherine Hall and Keith McClelland, *Race, Nation and Empire: Making Histories, 1970 to the Present* (Manchester: Manchester University Press 2012), pp. 216–236; Geoff Eley, "Empire by land or sea? Germany's imperial imaginary, 1840–1945", in Geoff Eley and Bradley D. Naranch (eds), *German Cultures of Colonialism: Race, Nation and Globalization, 1884–1945* (forthcoming); Geoff Eley, "Empire, Ideology and the East: Thoughts on Nazism's spatial imaginary" (forthcoming).
21. Quoted in Eley, "Empire by land or sea?", p. 13 of manuscript shared by author. On "liberal imperialists" such as Rohrbach, see Dehio, *Germany and World Politics in the Twentieth Century*.
22. David Calleo, *The German Problem Reconsidered: Germany and the World Order, 1870 to the Present* (London/New York/Melbourne: Cambridge University Press 1978), p. 37.
23. Eley, "Empire by land or sea", p. 19.
24. Craig, *Germany, 1866–1945*, p. 119.
25. Ibid., pp. 116–7.
26. Prince Hohenlohe-Schillingsfürst quoted in Simms, *Europe: The Struggle for Supremacy*, p. 250.
27. Hans-Ulrich Wehler, *Bismarck und der Imperialismus* (Cologne: Kiepenhauer & Witsch, 1969).
28. Craig, *Germany, 1866–1945*, p. 117.
29. Ibid., p. 303.
30. See Sean McMeekin, *The Berlin-Baghdad Express: The Ottoman Empire and Germany's Bid for World Power, 1898–1918* (Harmondsworth: Penguin, 2011).
31. Max Weber, "The Nation State and Economic Policy", in Peter Lassmann and Ronald Speirs (eds), *Weber: Political Writings* (Cambridge: Cambridge University Press, 1994), pp. 1–28, here p. 25.
32. Dehio, *Germany and World Politics in the Twentieth Century*, p. 88.
33. Ibid., p. 16.
34. Simms, *Europe: The Struggle for Supremacy*, p. 268.
35. Letter by Lord Odo Russell, British ambassador to Germany, to Lord Granville,

British foreign secretary, 11 February 1873, available at http://germanhistorydocs.ghi-dc.org/sub_document.cfm?document_id=1853

36. Craig, *Germany, 1866–1945*, p. 309.
37. Ibid., p. 308.
38. George F. Kennan, *The Fateful Alliance: France, Russia, and the Coming of the First World War* (New York: Pantheon Books, 1984).
39. Eyre Crowe, Memorandum on the Present State of British Relations with France and Germany, 1 January 1907, reproduced in G. P. Gooch and Harold Temperley (eds), *British Documents on the Origins of the War, Volume III: The Testing of the Entente, 1904—6* (London: His Majesty's Stationery Office, 1928).
40. Christopher Clark, *Sleepwalkers: How Europe Went to War in 1914* (London: Allen Lane, 2013), p. 158.
41. David Blackbourn, *History of Germany, 1780–1918: The long nineteenth century* (Oxford: Blackwell, 1997), p. xv.
42. Quoted in Kissinger, *Diplomacy*, p. 267.
43. Adam Tooze, *The Wages of Destruction: The Making and Breaking of the Nazi Economy* (Harmondsworth: Penguin, 2007), p. 3; Gottfried Niedhart, "Außenminister Stresemann und die ökonomische Variante deutscher Machtpolitik", in Karl Heinrich Pohl (ed.), *Politiker und Bürger: Gustav Stresemann und seine Zeit* (Göttingen: Vandenhoeck & Ruprecht, 2002), pp. 229–42.
44. Tooze, *The Wages of Destruction*, p. xxiv.
45. See Mearsheimer *The Tragedy of Great Power Politics*, p. 316.
46. See Mark Mazower, *Hitler's Empire: Nazi Rule in Occupied Europe* (Harmondsworth: Penguin, 2008).
47. Craig, *Germany, 1866–1945*, p. 745.
48. Taylor, *The Struggle for Mastery in Europe, 1848–1918*, p. xxxvi.
49. Calleo, *The German Problem Reconsidered*, p. 2.
50. Wehler, *Bismarck und der Imperialismus.*
51. David Blackbourn and Geoff Eley, *Mythen deutscher Geschichtsschreibung: Die gescheiterte bürgerliche Revolution von 1848* (Munich: Ullstein, 1980).
52. Helmut Walser Smith, "Where the *Sonderweg* debate left us", *German Studies Review*, 31: 2, May 2008, pp. 225–240, here p. 227.
53. Walser Smith, "Where the *Sonderweg* debate left us", p. 232.
54. Mearsheimer, *The Tragedy of Great Power Politics*, p. 2.
55. Ibid., p. 169.
56. Ibid., p. 183.
57. Calleo, *The German Problem Reconsidered*, p. 7.

2. IDEALISM AND REALISM

1. Eckart Conze, Norbert Frei, Peter Hayes and Moshe Zimmermann, *Das Amt und*

die Vergangenheit: Deutsche Diplomaten im Dritten Reich und in der Bundesrepublik (Munich: Karl Blessing Verlag, 2010).

2. On these perceived continuities between the Third Reich and the Federal Republic, see Hans Kundnani, *Utopia or Auschwitz: Germany's 1968 Generation and the Holocaust* (London/New York: Hurst/Columbia University Press, 2009).
3. Christopher Hill, *The actors in Europe's foreign policy* (London: Routledge, 1996), Amazon Kindle edition, Location 430.
4. See for example Eckart Conze, *Die Suche nach Sicherheit: Eine Geschichte der Bundesrepublik von 1949 bis in die Gegenwart* (Munich: Siedler Verlag, 2009).
5. See for example Beverly Crawford, "The Normative Power of a Normal State: Power and Revolutionary Vision in Germany's Post-Wall Foreign Policy", *German Politics and Society*, 28: 2, Summer 2010, pp. 165–184.
6. Hanns W. Maull, "Germany and Japan: The New Civilian Powers", *Foreign Affairs*, Winter 1990/91, available at http://www.foreignaffairs.com/articles/46262/hanns-w-maull/germany-and-japan-the-new-civilian-powers
7. Richard Rosecrance, *The Rise of the Trading State: Commerce and Conquest in the Modern World* (New York: Basic Books, 1986).
8. See for example Michael Staack, *Handelsstaat Deutschland: Deutsche Außenpolitik in einem neuen internationalen System* (Paderborn: Schöningh, 2000).
9. See Hanns W. Maull, "Zivilmacht Bundesrepublik Deutschland. Vierzehn Thesen für eine neue deutsche Außenpolitik", *Europa-Archiv*, 47, 1992, pp. 269–278.
10. Quoted in Ryan Lizza, "The Consequentialist" *New Yorker*, 2 May 2011, available at http://www.newyorker.com/reporting/2011/05/02/110502fa_fact_lizza
11. Walter Russell Mead, *Special Providence: American foreign policy and how it changed the world* (New York/London: Routledge, 2002), pp. 77–8.
12. Konrad Adenauer, "The German Problem, a World Problem", *Foreign Affairs*, October 1962, available at http://www.foreignaffairs.com/articles/23447/konrad-adenauer/the-german-problem-a-world-problem
13. Schuman Declaration, 9 May 1950, available at http://europa.eu/about-eu/basic-information/symbols/europe-day/schuman-declaration/index_en.htm
14. See Dietrich Thränhardt, *Geschichte der Bundesrepublik Deutschland* (Frankfurt/Main: Suhrkamp, 1996), p. 80.
15. Ibid., p. 79.
16. Peter Pulzer, *German Politics, 1945–1995* (Oxford: Oxford University Press, 1995) p. 59.
17. Stanley Hoffmann, "Obstinate or Obsolete? The Fate of the Nation-State and the Case of Western Europe", *Daedalus*, 95, Summer 1966, pp. 862–915, here p. 894.
18. Timothy Garton Ash, "The crisis of Europe", *Foreign Affairs*, September/October 2012, available at http://www.foreignaffairs.com/articles/138010/timothy-garton-ash/the-crisis-of-europe

19. Henry Kissinger, *Years of Upheaval* (London: Simon and Schuster, 2011), p. 144.
20. Egon Bahr, *Zu meiner Zeit* (Munich: Karl Blessing Verlag, 1996), p. 46.
21. Ibid., p. 66.
22. Ibid., p. 156.
23. Ibid., p. 157.
24. Kissinger, *Years of Upheaval*, p. 147.
25. Gordon A. Craig, "Did Ostpolitik work?" *Foreign Affairs*, January/February 1994, available at http://www.foreignaffairs.com/articles/49450/gordon-a-craig/did-ostpolitik-work
26. Kissinger, *Years of Upheaval*, p. 146.
27. Ibid.
28. Ibid., p. 148.
29. Ibid., p. 735.
30. Ibid., p. 736.
31. Ibid.
32. Egon Bahr, *"Das musst du erzählen." Erinnerungen an Willy Brandt* (Munich: Propyläen, 2013), p. 76.
33. Timothy Garton Ash, *In Europe's Name: Germany and the Divided Continent* (London: Jonathan Cape, 1993), p. 75.
34. On the Christian Democrats' private intelligence service, see Stefanie Waske, "Die Verschwörung gegen Brandt", *Die Zeit*, 2 December 2012, available at http://www.zeit.de/2012/49/Spionage-CDU-CSU-Willy-Brandt
35. See Justin Vaïsse, *Neoconservatism: The biography of a movement* (Cambridge: Harvard University Press, 2010), p. 100.
36. See Heinrich August Winkler, "Power, Morality, and Human Rights. The role of values and interests in Germany's foreign policy", *IP Journal*, 15 July 2013, available at https://ip-journal.dgap.org/en/ip-journal/topics/power-morality-and-human-rights
37. Craig, "Did Ostpolitik work?"
38. Winkler, "Power, Morality, and Human Rights".
39. Craig, "Did Ostpolitik work?"
40. Andrei S. Markovits and Philip S. Gorski, *The German Left: Red, Green and Beyond* (Cambridge: Polity, 1993), p. 56.
41. On the Federal Republic as a "trading state" during this period, see Gunther Hellmann, *Deutsche Außenpolitik: Eine Einführung* (Wiesbaden: VS Verlag für Wissenschaften, 2006), pp. 95–96.
42. For a fuller discussion of the Federal Republic's engagement with the Nazi past, and in particular the role of the so-called 1968 generation in it, see Kundnani, *Utopia or Auschwitz*.
43. See Peter Novick, *The Holocaust and Collective Memory*, (London: Bloomsbury, 1999).
44. Jeffrey Herf, *Divided Memory: The Nazi Past in the two Germanys* (Cambridge, Massachusetts: Harvard University Press, 1997), p. 345.

45. Ibid.
46. Ibid.
47. Ernst Nolte, "Vergangenheit, die nicht vergehen will", in *"Historikerstreit": Die Dokumentation der Kontroverse um die Einzigartigkeit der nationalsozialistischen Judenvernichtung* (Munich: Piper, 1987), pp. 39–47, here p. 45.
48. Nolte writes that "normally every past passes" and that a *Schlußstrich* would mean that "this German past would no longer fundamentally differ from other pasts." Nolte, "Vergangenheit, die nicht vergehen will", in *"Historikerstreit"*, pp. 39, 40.
49. Charles S. Maier, *The Unmasterable Past: History, Holocaust and German National Identity* (Cambridge, Massachusetts: Harvard University Press, 1997), p. 2.
50. Michael Wolffsohn, *Ewige Schuld? 40 Jahre deutsche-jüdische-israelische Beziehungen* (Munich: Piper, 1988), p. 42. For a fuller discussion of how Schmidt's remarks illustrated how the collective memory of the Holocaust acted as a "cultural constraint" on West German foreign policy, see Jeffrey K. Olick and Daniel Levy, "Collective Memory and Cultural Constraint: Holocaust Myth and Rationality in German Politics", *American Sociological Review*, 62, December 1997, pp. 921–936.
51. Joschka Fischer, "Wir Kinder der Kapitulanten", *Die Zeit*, 10 May 1985, available at http://www.zeit.de/1985/19/wir-kinder-der-kapitulanten

3. CONTINUITY AND CHANGE

1. Kurt Georg Kiesinger, Rede beim Staatsakt der Bundesregierung zum Tag der Deutschen Einheit im Bundestag, 17. Juni 1967.
2. Stanley Hoffmann, "French Dilemmas and Strategies in the New Europe", Harvard University Center for European Studies Working Paper Series Collection 152, 1992. (Reprinted in: Robert Keohane, Joseph S. Nye and Stanley Hoffmann [eds], *After the Cold War: International Institutions and State Strategies in Europe, 1989–1991* [Cambridge: Harvard University Press, 1993], pp. 127–147.)
3. See Schwarz, *Die Zentralmacht Europas*.
4. See for example John J. Mearsheimer, "Back to the future: instability in Europe after the Cold War", *International Security*, 15: 1, Summer 1990, pp. 5–56.
5. Adrian Hyde-Price, *Germany and European Order: Enlarging NATO and the EU* (Manchester: Manchester University Press, 2000), p. 107.
6. Margaret Thatcher, *The Downing Street Years* (London: Harper Collins, 1993), p. 791.
7. Patrick Salmon, Keith Hamilton and Stephen Twigge (eds), *Documents on British Policy Overseas, Series III, Volume VII: German Reunification 1989–1990* (London: Routledge, 2009), p. 217.
8. Geir Lundested, *The United States and Western Europe Since 1945: From 'Empire' by Invitation to Transatlantic Drift* (Oxford: Oxford University Press, 2005), p. 9.
9. See Hoffmann, "French Dilemmas and Strategies in the New Europe".

10. Quoted in David Marsh, *The Euro: The Politics of the New Global Currency* (New Haven and London: Yale University Press, 2009), p. 135.
11. Thatcher, *The Downing Street Years*, p. 791.
12. See Marsh, *The Euro*, pp. 53–57.
13. Ibid., p. 137
14. Ibid.
15. Theodor Adorno, "Was heißt: Aufarbeitung der Vergangenheit?" in *Eingriffe: Neun kritische Modelle* (Frankfurt/Main: Suhrkamp, 1963), pp. 125–146, here p. 137.
16. Christian Meier, "Wir sind ja keine normale Nation", *Die Zeit*, 21 September 1990.
17. Jürgen Habermas, *Die nachholende Revolution* (Frankfurt/Main: Suhrkamp, 1990), p. 152.
18. Ibid.
19. Ibid.
20. Jürgen Habermas, "1989 im Schatten von 1945. Zur Normalität einer künftigen Berliner Republik", in *Die Normalität einer Berliner Republik* (Frankfurt/Main: Suhrkamp, 1995), pp. 67–188, here p. 171.
21. Jürgen Habermas, "Der Golf-Krieg als Katalysator einer neuen deutschen Normalität?" in *Vergangenheit als Zukunft: Das alte Deutschland im neuen Europa?* (Munich: Piper, 1993), pp. 10–44, here p. 42.
22. Jürgen Habermas, "Die Asyl-Debatte" in Habermas, *Vergangenheit als Zukunft*, pp. 159–186, here p. 180.
23. Jürgen Habermas, "1989 im Schatten von 1945. Zur Normalität einer künftigen Berliner Republik", in Jürgen Habermas, *Die Normalität einer Berliner Republik* (Frankfurt/Main: Suhrkamp, 1995), pp. 167–188, here p. 172.
24. Marsh, *The Euro*, p. 133.
25. Quoted in Ibid., p. 132.
26. Ibid., p. 132.
27. Hoffmann, "French Dilemmas and Strategies in the New Europe".
28. Jürgen Habermas, "Der DM-Nationalismus", *Die Zeit*, 30 March 1990, available at http://www.zeit.de/1990/14/der-dm-nationalismus
29. Mary Elise Sarotte, "Eurozone Crisis as Historical Legacy", *Foreign Affairs*, 29 September 2010, available at http://www.foreignaffairs.com/articles/66754/mary-elise-sarotte/eurozone-crisis-as-historical-legacy
30. Martin Feldstein, "EMU and International Conflict", *Foreign Affairs*, November/December 1997, available at http://www.foreignaffairs.com/articles/53576/martin-feldstein/emu-and-international-conflict
31. Habermas, *Vergangenheit als Zukunft*, p. 191.
32. Speech on 23 August 1990, quoted in Gunther Hellmann, Christian Weber and Frank Sauer (eds), *Die Semantik der neuen deutschen Außenpolitik: Eine Analyse des außenpolitischen Vokabulars seit Mitte der 1980er Jahre* (Wiesbaden: VS Verlag für Sozialwissenschaften 2008), p. 131.

33. Speech on 13 March 1991, quoted in Hellmann, Weber and Sauer, *Die Semantik der neuen deutschen Außenpolitik*, p. 132.
34. On "modified continuity", see Sebastian Harnisch and Hanns W. Maull, *Germany as a civilian power? The foreign policy of the Berlin Republic* (Manchester: Manchester University Press, 2001), p. 2.
35. See Ludger Volmer, *Die Grünen und die Außenpolitik: Ein schwieriges Verhältnis* (Münster: Verlag Westfäliges Dampfboot, 1998), especially pp. 493–496.
36. Hanns W. Maull, "'Zivilmacht': Karriere eines Begriffs" Abschiedsvorlesung am 3. Mai 2013, pp. 8–9, available at http://www.uni-trier.de/fileadmin/fb3/POL/Maull/Abschiedsvorlesung_Rev.pdf
37. Cohn-Bendit cited in Wolfgang Kraushaar, *Fischer in Frankfurt. Karriere einers Außenseiters* (Hamburg: Hamburger Edition, 2001), pp. 106–107.
38. Author interview with Joschka Fischer, Berlin, 1 September 2008.
39. On the effect of the Srebrenica massacre on Joschka Fischer's thinking, see Kundnani, *Utopia or Auschwitz*, pp. 240–244.
40. Author interview with Joschka Fischer, Berlin, 1 September 2008.
41. Winkler, *The Long Road West. Volume II*, p. 564.
42. See Jan-Werner Müller, *Another Country: German Intellectuals, Unification and National Identity* (New Haven/London: Yale University Press 2000), p. 269.
43. Martin Walser, "Die Banalität des Guten: Erfahrungen beim Verfassen einer Sonntagsrede aus Anlaß der Verleihung des Friedenspreis des Deutschen Buchhandels", in *Frankfurter Allgemeine Zeitung*, 12 October 1998. Reprinted in Frank Schirrmacher (ed.), *Die Walser-Bubis Debatte: Eine Dokumentation* (Frankfurt/Main: Suhrkamp, 1999), pp. 7–17.
44. Regierungserklärung des Bundeskanzlers am 10 November 1998 vor dem Deutschen Bundestag in Bonn.
45. See for example Patrick Bahners, "Total Normal. Vorsicht Falle: Die unbefangene Nation", *Frankfurter Allgemeine Zeitung*, 3 November 1998; Werner A. Perger, "Wir Unbefangenen", *Die Zeit*, 12 November 1998; "Total normal?" *Der Spiegel*, 30 November 1998.
46. On Fischer's emphasis on continuity in German foreign policy, see his interview with *Die Zeit* shortly after his appointment as foreign minister: "Ein Realo sieht die Welt", *Die Zeit*, 12 November 1998.
47. Michael Walzer, *Just and Unjust Wars* (New York: Basic Books, 2000), p. xii.
48. Paul Berman, *Power and the Idealists: The passion of Joschka Fischer, and its aftermath* (New York: Soft Skull Press, 2005), p. 91.
49. Roger Cohen, "Germany's Pragmatic Ex-Radical thinks globally", *New York Times*, 28 January 1999, available at http://www.nytimes.com/1999/01/28/world/germany-s-pragmatic-ex-radical-thinks-globally.html
50. Joschka Fischer, *Die rot-grünen Jahre: Deutsche Außenpolitik—vom Kosovo bis zum 11. September* (Cologne: Kiepenhauer und Witsch, 2007), p. 185.

51. Frank Schirrmacher, "Luftkampf. Deutschlands Anteil am Krieg", *Frankfurter Allgemeine Zeitung*, 17 April 1999, available at http://www.seiten.faz-archiv.de/faz/19990417/f19990417proz—100.html
52. Author interview with Gerhard Schröder, Berlin, 27 August 2008.
53. Rede von Bundeskanzler Gerhard Schröder anlässlich der 35. Münchener Tagung für Sicherheitspolitik, Munich, 6 February 1999.
54. Günter Joetze, *Der letzte Krieg in Europa? Das Kosovo und die deutsche Politik* (Stuttgart: Deutsche Verlags-Anstalt, 2001), p. 8.
55. Quoted in Ibid., p. 1.
56. Winkler, *The Long Road West. Volume II*, p. 587.

4. PERPETRATORS AND VICTIMS

1. Steven Erlanger, "Germans Vote in a Tight Election in Which Bush, Hitler and Israel Became Key Issues", *New York Times*, 22 September 2002, available at http://www.nytimes.com/2002/09/22/world/germans-vote-tight-election-which-bush-hitler-israel-became-key-issues.html
2. Robert A. Pape, "Soft Balancing against the United States", *International Security*, Vol. 30, No. 1 (Summer 2005), pp. 7–45. Pape defines "soft balancing" against the United States as "the use of nonmilitary tools to delay, frustrate, and undermine aggressive unilateral U.S. military policies".
3. Stephen F. Szabo, *Parting Ways: The Crisis in German-American Relations* (Washington, D.C.: Brookings Institution, 2004), p. 1.
4. Quoted in Ibid., pp. 129, 79.
5. Szabo, *Parting Ways*, p. 6.
6. Ronald D. Asmus, "Rebuilding the Atlantic Alliance", *Foreign Affairs*, September/October 2003, available at http://www.foreignaffairs.com/articles/59180/ronald-d-asmus/rebuilding-the-atlantic-alliance
7. See Steven Erlanger, "Stance on Bush Policy Could Swing Election in Germany", *New York Times*, 9 September 2002.
8. US claims about the existence of weapons of mass destruction in Iraq rested to a large extent on a source known as "Curveball" who was controlled by the German foreign intelligence service, the *Bundesnachrichtendienst* (BND). "Curveball", whose real name was Rafid Ahmed Alwan, was a Iraqi defector who had arrived in Germany in 1999 and claimed asylum. A chemical engineer, he falsely claimed he had worked at mobile biological weapons laboratories in Iraq. Although the BND passed on reports on Curveball's claims to the American Defence Intelligence Agency (DIA), it did not allow the DIA or other American intelligence agencies direct access to him.
9. Ibid.
10. Author interview with Gerhard Schröder, Berlin, 27 August 2008.

11. See "Das Comeback des Kanzlers", *Der Spiegel*, 16 September 2002, available at http://www.spiegel.de/spiegel/print/d-25180468.html
12. Author interview with Joschka Fischer, Berlin, 1 September 2008; John Hooper, "Fischer rejects chancellor's 'German way'", *Guardian*, 15 October 2002, available at http://www.theguardian.com/world/2002/oct/15/germany.johnhooper
13. Michael R. Gordon, "German intelligence gave U.S. Iraqi defense plan, report says", *New York Times*, 27 February 2006, available at http://www.nytimes.com/2006/02/27/politics/27germans.html?pagewanted=all&_r=0; Richard Bernstein and Michael R. Gordon, "Berlin file says Germany's spies aided U.S. in Iraq", *New York Times*, 2 March 2006, available at http://www.nytimes.com/2006/03/02/international/europe/02germany.html?hp&ex=1141362000&en=6efea12061967fbb&ei=5094&partner=homepage; Michael R. Gordon and General Bernard E. Trainor, *Cobra II: The Inside Story of the Invasion and Occupation of Iraq* (New York: Vintage, 2007), pp. 140–142.
14. Szabo, *Parting Ways*, p. 1.
15. Gerhard Schröder, *Entscheidungen: Mein Leben in der Politik* (Hamburg: Hoffmann und Campe, 2006), p. 247.
16. Francois Heisbourg, "The French-German Duo and the Search for a New European Security Model", *International Spectator*, 3, 2004.
17. Szabo, *Parting Ways*, p. 10.
18. See for example Ruth Wittlinger, "Taboo or Tradition? The 'Germans as victims' theme in the Federal Republic until the mid-1990s", in Bill Niven (ed.) *Germans as victims: Remembering the past in contemporary Germany* (Basingstoke: Palgrave Macmillan, 2006), pp. 62–75.
19. Eric Langenbacher, "The Mastered Past? Collective Memory Trends in Germany since Unification", in Jeffrey Anderson and Eric Langenbacher (eds), *From the Bonn to the Berlin Republic: Germany at the Twentieth Anniversary of Unification* (New York/Oxford: Berghahn, 2010), pp. 63–89, here, p. 63.
20. Ibid.
21. Christopher Rhoads, "A Flood of War Memories Spur Germany's Current Iraq Stance", *Wall Street Journal*, 25 February 2003, available at http://online.wsj.com/article/0,,SB1054786129132649000,00.html
22. Ibid.
23. Jörg Friedrich, *Der Brand: Deutschland im Bombenkrieg 1940–1945* (Munich: Propyläen, 2002).
24. Bill Niven, "Introduction: German Victimhood at the Turn of the Millennium", in Niven (ed.), *Germans as Victims*, pp. 1–25, here p. 14.
25. See Andreas Huyssen, "Air War Legacies: From Dresden to Baghdad" in Niven (ed.), *Germans as Victims*, pp. 181–193, here p. 188.
26. Niven (ed.), *Germans as Victims*, p. 182. See also Richard Bernstein, "Germans Revisit War's Agony, Ending a Taboo", *New York Times*, 15 March 2003, available at http://www.nytimes.com/2003/03/15/international/europe/15DRES.html

27. Rhoads, "Behind Iraq Stance in Germany: Flood of War Memories".
28. On Auschwitz and Dresden, see George Packer, "Embers", *New Yorker*, 1 February 2010, available at http://www.newyorker.com/reporting/2010/02/01/100201 fa_fact_packer
29. The following section draws extensively on arguments I have made elsewhere. See Hans Kundnani, "The Concept of "Normality" in German Foreign Policy since Unification", *German Politics and Society*, Volume 30, Issue 2, Summer 2012, pp. 38–58.
30. Rede von Bundeskanzler Gerhard Schröder anlässlich der 35. Münchener Tagung für Sicherheitspolitik, Munich, 6 February 1999.
31. Speech on 29 September 2010, quoted in Hellmann, Weber and Sauer, *Die Semantik der neuen deutschen Außenpolitik*, p. 133.
32. Author interview with Gerhard Schröder, Berlin, 27 August 2008.
33. Egon Bahr, "Die 'Normaliseriung' der deutschen Außenpolitik: Mündige Partnerschaft statt bequemer Vormundschaft", *Internationale Politik*, 54, 1, 1999, pp. 41–52.
34. Ibid., p. 42.
35. Ibid., p. 41.
36. Ibid., p. 44.
37. See for example Matthias Geyer, Dirk Kurbjuweit and Cordt Schnibben, *Operation Rot-Grün: Geschichte eines politischen Abenteuers* (Munich/Hamburg: Deutsche Verlags-Anstalt/Spiegel-Buchverlag, 2005), p. 202.
38. Author interview with Gerhard Schröder, Berlin, 27 August 2008.
39. Egon Bahr, *Der deutsche Weg: Selbstverständlich und normal* (Munich: Blessing, 2003), p. 155.
40. Ibid., pp. 136–7.
41. Ibid.
42. Ibid.
43. Ibid., p. 139.
44. Ibid., p. 146.
45. Ibid., p. 103.
46. Ibid., pp. 102–103.
47. Ibid., p. 9.
48. Ibid., pp. 135.
49. Author interview with Gerhard Schröder, Berlin, 27 August 2008.
50. Ibid.
51. Ibid. See also Schröder, *Entscheidungen*, p. 246.
52. Steven Erlanger, "German Seeks A New Force Led by NATO In Macedonia", *New York Times*, 9 September 2001, available at http://www.nytimes.com/2001/09/09/world/german-seeks-a-new-force-led-by-nato-in-macedonia.html
53. Stefan Kornelius, "Der unerklärte Krieg. Deutschlands Selbstbetrug in Afghanistan", Körber Stiftung, June 2009, pp. 39–40.

54. Author interview with senior British officer, London, 30 October 2007.
55. Timo Noetzel and Thomas Rid, "Germany's Options in Afghanistan", *Survival*, 51: 5, October–November 2009, pp. 71–90; Timo Noetzel, "Germany's small war in Afghanistan: Military Learning amid Politico-strategic Inertia", *Contemporary Security Policy*, 31: 3, December 2010, pp. 486–508; Timo Noetzel, "The German politics of war: Kunduz and the war in Afghanistan", *International Affairs*, 87: 2, 2011, pp. 397–417.
56. Sozialwissenschaftliches Institut der Bundeswehr, Sicherheits- und verteidigungspolitisches Meinungsklima in Deutschland. Ergebnisse der Bevölkerungsbefragung Oktober/November 2009, Kurzbericht, January 2010, pp. 33–37.
57. Kornelius, *Der unerklärte Krieg*, p. 9.
58. Rajiv Chandrasekaran, "Decision on Airstrike in Afghanistan Was Based Largely on Sole Informant's Assessment", *Washington Post*, 6 September 2009, available at http://www.washingtonpost.com/wp-dyn/content/article/2009/09/05/AR2009090502832.html
59. On the effect of the Kunduz bombing on German Afghanistan policy, see Timo Noetzel, "The German politics of war: Kunduz and the war in Afghanistan", *International Affairs*, 87, 2, 2011, pp. 397–417, available at http://www.chathamhouse.org/sites/default/files/public/International%20Affairs/2011/87_2noetzel.pdf
60. Thomas Schmid, "Im Wohnzimmer durch die Welt", *Internationale Politik*, November/December 2010, available at https://zeitschrift-ip.dgap.org/de/ip-die-zeitschrift/archiv/jahrgang-2010/november-dezember/im-wohnzimmer-durch-die-welt.

5. ECONOMICS AND POLITICS

1. Quoted in Marcus Walker, "Is Germany Turning into the Strong, Silent Type?", *Wall Street Journal*, 27 June 2011, available at http://online.wsj.com/article/SB10001424052702304259304576373281798293222.html
2. Bodo Hombach, *The Politics of the New Centre* (Cambridge: Polity, 2000), p. 105.
3. On the effects of the Schröder reforms, see Sebastian Dullien, "German reforms as a blueprint for Europe?" in Stefan Collignon and Piero Esposito, *Competitiveness in the European Economy* (London: Routledge, 2014), pp. 146–60.
4. Margit Feher, "Audi Expands Hungary Plant to Make Model A3 Limousine", *Wall Street Journal*, 12 June 2013, available at http://blogs.wsj.com/emergingeurope/2013/06/12/car-maker-audi-expands-hungary-plant-to-make-model-a3-limousine/
5. "Europe's future in an age of austerity", Centre for European Reform conference report, Ditchley Park, Oxfordshire, 9–10 November 2012, p. 6, available at http://www.cer.org.uk/sites/default/files/publications/attachments/pdf/2012/ditchley_event_rpt14dec12–6728.pdf

6. Anke Hassel, "The Paradox of Liberalization. Understanding dualism and the recovery of the German political economy", LSE discussion paper, September 2011, p. 12, available at http://www.lse.ac.uk/europeanInstitute/LEQS/LEQSPaper42.pdf
7. International Labor Organization, Global Wage Report 2010/11, December 2010, available at http://www.ilo.org/wcmsp5/groups/public/@dgreports/@dcomm/@publ/documents/publication/wcms_145265.pdf
8. Dullien, "German reforms as a blueprint for Europe?", p. 151.
9. On productivity growth in France and Germany, see Dullien, "German reforms as a blueprint for Europe?", pp. 152–153.
10. Adam S. Posen, "Getting Germany Past Internal Devaluation", Peterson Institute for International Economics, 9 June 2013, available at http://www.iie.com/publications/opeds/oped.cfm?ResearchID=2424
11. World Bank figures, available at http://data.worldbank.org/indicator/NE.EXP.GNFS.ZS?page=2
12. Simon Tilford, "How to save the euro", Centre for European Reform, September 2010, p. 3, available at http://www.cer.org.uk/sites/default/files/publications/attachments/pdf/2011/essay_euro_tilford_14sept10–196.pdf
13. Remark by Arndt Ellinghorst, head of automotive research at Credit Suisse, Bloomberg German Economic Summit, London, 9 July 2012.
14. Raghuram Rajan, *Fault Lines: How Hidden Fractures Still Threaten the World Economy* (Princeton/Oxford: Princeton University Press, 2010), p. 47.
15. Philip Whyte, "Why Germany is not a model for the eurozone", Centre for European Reform, October 2010, p. 7, available at http://www.cer.org.uk/sites/default/files/publications/attachments/pdf/2011/essay_germany_eurozone_oct10–189.pdf
16. Adam Tooze, "Germany's unsustainable growth", *Foreign Affairs*, September/October 2012, available at http://www.foreignaffairs.com/articles/137834/adam-tooze/germanys-unsustainable-growth
17. Posen, "Getting Germany Past Internal Devaluation".
18. Paul Krugman, "Can Europe be saved?", *New York Times*, 12 January 2011, available at http://www.nytimes.com/2011/01/16/magazine/16Europe-t.html?pagewanted=all&_r=0
19. Martin Wolf, "The German model is not for export", *Financial Times*, 7 May 2013, available at http://www.ft.com/cms/s/0/aacd1be0-b637–11e2–93ba-00144feabdc0.html
20. Moravcsik, "Europe after the Crisis", *Foreign Affairs*, May/June 2012, available at http://www.foreignaffairs.com/articles/137421/andrew-moravcsik/europe-after-the-crisis
21. Tilford, "How to save the euro", p. 3.
22. Simon Tilford, "Will the Eurozone Crack?", Centre for European Reform,

September 2006, available at http://www.cer.org.uk/sites/default/files/publications/attachments/pdf/2011/p_688_eurozone_crack_42–892.pdf

23. Author interview with German official, Berlin, 11 April 2012.
24. See Dorothee Tschampa, Alexandra Ho and Christoph Rauwald, "Mercedes Revamps the S-Class to Lure China's Wealthy Buyers", *Business Week*, 13 May 2013, available at http://www.businessweek.com/articles/2013–05–16/mercedes-revamps-the-s-class-to-lure-chinas-wealthy-buyers
25. Moravcsik, "Europe after the Crisis".
26. See Hans Kundnani, "Russia or the West?" *Prospect*, 25 October 2008, available at http://www.prospectmagazine.co.uk/magazine/russiaorthewest/
27. Stephen F. Szabo, "Can Berlin and Washington Agree on Russia?", *Washington Quarterly*, 32:4, October 2009, pp. 23–41, available at http://www.gmfus.org/wp-content/files, here p. 30.
28. See Alexander Rahr, "Germany and Russia: a special relationship", *Washington Quarterly*, 30:2, Spring 2007, pp. 137–145.
29. See Schröder, *Entscheidungen*, pp. 139–40.
30. Ibid., p. 143.
31. "Merkel in China: 'Mut zu kritischen Tönen'", *Frankfurter Allgemeine Zeitung*, 23 May 2006, available at http://www.faz.net/aktuell/politik/ausland/merkel-in-china-mut-zu-kritischen-toenen-1327483.html
32. "Chinas Regierung lässt jubeln", *Frankfurter Allgemeine Zeitung*, 26 January 2008, available at http://www.seiten.faz-archiv.de/faz/20080126/fd2200801261546 704. html
33. Felix Heiduk, "Conflicting images? Germany and the Rise of China", *German Politics*, Volume 23, Issue 1–2, 2014, pp. 118–133.
34. Author interviews with Chinese officials, Beijing, March 2012.
35. Gerd Appenzeller, "Die Deutschland-AG ist wieder da", *Der Tagesspiegel*, 5 March 2013, available at http://www.tagesspiegel.de/wirtschaft/exporthilfe-die-deutschland-ag-ist-wieder-da/7882394.html
36. Stephen F. Szabo, "Can Berlin and Washington Agree on Russia?", p. 24.
37. Schröder, *Entscheidungen*, p. 141.
38. Der Spiegel, 10 May 2010. As far as I am aware, Lambsdorff was the first to use this phrase. Quoted in "Duell der Titanen".
39. For the full text of the judgment, see http://www.bundesverfassungsgericht.de/entscheidungen/es20090630_2bve000208en.html
40. On "attritional" multilateralism, see Timothy Garton Ash, "Germany's Choice", *Foreign Affairs*, July/August 1994, p. 71, available at http://www.foreignaffairs.com/articles/50101/timothy-garton-ash/germanys-choice
41. On the Chinese perception of a "new imperialism", see David Shambaugh, "Coping with a Conflicted China", *Washington Quarterly*, 34, 1, Winter 2011, p. 11, available at https://csis.org/files/publication/twq11wintershambaugh.pdf

42. See for example Sebastian Dullien, "Wieso die Schuldenbremse Wahnsinn ist", Spiegel Online, 9 February 2009, available at http://www.spiegel.de/wirtschaft/kommentar-wieso-die-schuldenbremse-wahnsinn-ist-a-606389.html
43. Tooze, "Germany's unsustainable growth".
44. Paul Krugman, *End this Depression Now!* (New York: Norton, 2012), p. xxii.
45. "'It Doesn't Exist!' Germany's outspoken finance minister on the hopeless search for 'the Great Rescue Plan'", *Newsweek*, 5 December 2008, available at http://www.thedailybeast.com/newsweek/2008/12/05/it-doesn-t-exist.html
46. Paul Krugman, "The economic consequences of Herr Steinbrueck", *New York Times*, 11 December 2008, available at http://krugman.blogs.nytimes.com/2008/12/11/the-economic-consequences-of-herr-steinbrueck/?_r=1
47. Quoted in Marcus Walker, "Is Germany Turning into the Strong, Silent Type?"
48. Maull, "'Zivilmacht': Karriere eines Begriffs", p 20.
49. On the history of anti-Americanism in German thinking, see Dan Diner, *Feindbild Amerika: Über die Beständigkeit eines Ressentiments* (Munich: Propyläen, 2002).
50. On the re-emergence of the idea of "Modell Deutschland" after 2008 see Andreas Rödder, "'Modell Deutschland' 1950–2011. Konjunkturen einer bundesdeutschen Ordnungsvorstellung", in Tilman Mayer, Karl-Heinz Paqué and Andreas H. Apelt, *Modell Deutschland* (Berlin: Duncker & Humblot, 2013), pp. 39–51.

6. EUROPE AND THE WORLD

1. George Soros, "Why Germany Should Lead or Leave", Project Syndicate, 8 September 2012, available at http://www.project-syndicate.org/commentary/why-germany-should-lead-or-leave-by-george-soros
2. Jack Ewing, "In Euro Crisis, Fingers Can Point in All Directions", *New York Times*, 24 August 2012, available at http://www.nytimes.com/2012/08/25/business/global/in-euro-crisis-plenty-of-blame-to-go-around.html?pagewanted=all
3. Joschka Fischer, "Frau Germania", *Süddeutsche Zeitung*, 29 March 2010, available at http://www.sueddeutsche.de/politik/merkel-und-europa-frau-germania-1.10508
4. On asymmetric adjustment within the eurozone, see Paul de Grauwe, "In search of symmetry in the eurozone", Centre for European Policy Studies, May 2012, available at http://www.ceps.eu/book/search-symmetry-eurozone
5. "'Politik zum Schieflachen'. Interview mit Helmut Schmidt", *Cicero*, June 2010, available at http://www.cicero.de/97.php?ress_id=4&item=5147
6. "'Wir müssen wieder Zuversicht geben.' Helmut Kohl über eine Außenpolitik, der es an Verlässlichkeit mangelt", *Internationale Politik*, September/October 2011, available at https://zeitschrift-ip.dgap.org/de/ip-die-zeitschrift/archiv/jahrgang-2011/september-oktober,„wir-müssen-wieder-zuversicht-geben"

7. See "Shaping Globalization—Expanding Partnerships—Sharing Responsibility. A strategy paper by the German Government", 2012, available at http://www.auswaertiges-amt.de/cae/servlet/contentblob/616584/publicationFile/167908/Gestaltungsmaechtekonzept%20engl.pdf
8. UniCredit Economics Research, UniCredit Weekly Focus, No. 12, 12 April 2012, available at https://www.research.unicreditgroup.eu/DocsKey/economics_docs_2012_125939.ashx?KEY=C814QI31EjqIm_1zIJDBJGvd-rOCUpzh2jykB-Gfl5A%3D&EXT=pdf
9. See Nele Noesselt, "Strategiewechsel in der chinesischen Europapolitik: Umweg über Deutschland?", German Institute for Global and Area Studies, 2011, available at http://www.giga-hamburg.de/dl/download.php?d=/content/publikationen/pdf/gf_asien_1106.pdf
10. Author interview with Chinese official, Beijing, March 2012.
11. Martin Wolf, "China and Germany unite to impose global deflation", *Financial Times*, 16 March 2010, available at http://www.ft.com/cms/s/0/cd01f69e-3134-11df-8e6f-00144feabdc0.html
12. Deutsch-Chinesisches Kommuniqué, 16 July 2010, available at http://www.bundesregierung.de/Content/DE/Artikel/2010/07/2010-07-16-deutsch-chinesisches-kommunique.html
13. Interview on 5 August 2010, quoted in Jana Randow and Holger Elfes, "Germany Ignores Soros as Exports Boom at Consumers' Expense", Bloomberg, 18 August 2010, available at http://www.bloomberg.com/news/2010-08-17/germany-ignores-soros-as-exports-drive-record-growth-at-consumers-expense.html
14. Author interview with Chinese analyst, Beijing, March 2012.
15. See for example Ulrike Guérot, "Eine deutsche Versuchung: östliche Horizonte?", *Aus Politik und Zeitgeschichte*, 10, 2012, 5 March 2012, available at http://www.bpb.de/apuz/75786/eine-deutsche-versuchung-oestliche-horizonte?p=all
16. Wolfgang Proissl, "Why Germany fell out of love with Europe", *Bruegel*, July 2010, p. 8, available at http://www.bruegel.org/publications/publication-detail/publication/417-why-germany-fell-out-of-love-with-europe/
17. On Merkel's thinking during this period, see Stefan Kornelius, *Angela Merkel: Die Kanzlerin und ihre Welt* (Hamburg: Hoffmann und Campe, 2013), pp. 261–267.
18. Paul Krugman, "What ails Europe?", *New York Times*, 26 February 2012, available at http://www.nytimes.com/2012/02/27/opinion/krugman-what-ails-europe.html
19. Carsten Volkery, "Die Nacht, in der Merkel verlor", Spiegel Online, 29 June 2012, available at http://www.spiegel.de/politik/ausland/angela-merkel-erleidet-bei-eu-gipfel-niederlage-a-841653.html
20. Ferdinand Dyck, Martin Hesse and Alexander Jung, "The inflation monster: How Monetary Policy Threatens Savings", *Der Spiegel*, 8 October 2012, available at http://www.spiegel.de/international/europe/how-central-banks-are-threatening-the-savings-of-normal-germans-a-860021.html

21. Michael Steen, "Bond sceptic caught between devil and ECB", *Financial Times*, 18 September 2012, available at http://www.ft.com/cms/s/0/558d7996–01af-11e2–8aaa-00144feabdc0.html?siteedition=uk#axzz2dRrU57UQ. Weidmann's speech is available in English at http://www.bundesbank.de/Redaktion/EN/Reden/2012/2012_09_20_weidmann_money_creaktion_and_responsibility.html
22. This section draws extensively on arguments I have made elsewhere. See Hans Kundnani, "Europe and the Return of History", *Journal of Modern European History*, Volume 11, Number 3, August 2013, pp. 279–286.
23. "Towards a Genuine Economic and Monetary Union", 5 December 2012, available at http://www.consilium.europa.eu/uedocs/cms_Data/docs/pressdata/en/ec/134069.pdf
24. Speech at St. Antony's College, Oxford, 28 October 2012, available at http://www.sant.ox.ac.uk/esc/docs/SchäubleTranscript.pdf
25. See Thomas Klau, François Godement and José Ignacio Torreblanca, "Beyond Maastricht: A New Deal for the Eurozone", European Council on Foreign Relations, December 2010, available at http://www.ecfr.eu/page/-/ECFR26_BEYOND_MAASTRICHT_AW(2).pdf
26. Ian Traynor, "As the dust settles, a cold new Europe with Germany in charge will emerge", *Guardian*, 9 December 2011, available at http://www.guardian.co.uk/business/2011/dec/09/dust-settles-cold-europe-germany?newsfeed=true
27. Martin Wolf, "What Hollande Must Tell Germany", *Financial Times*, 8 May 2012, available at http://www.ft.com/cms/s/0/51bf429c-98f8–11e1–948a-00144feabdc0.html#axzz2HrtaTm4i
28. George Soros, "Remarks at the Festival of Economics, Trento Italy", 2 June 2012, available at http://www.georgesoros.com/interviews-speeches/entry/remarks_at_the_festival_of_economics_trento_italy/
29. Melissa Eddy, "Support Grows in Germany for Vote on Giving Up Power to European Bloc", *New York Times*, 18 August 2012, available at http://www.nytimes.com/2012/08/19/world/europe/referendum-on-europe-gains-support-in-germany.html?_r=0
30. Robert Gates, speech at the National Defense University, Washington, D.C., 23 February 2010, available at http://www.defense.gov/speeches/speech.aspx?speechid=1423
31. Robert Gates, speech in Brussels, 10 June 2011, available at http://www.defense.gov/speeches/speech.aspx?speechid=1581
32. Decisions about German arms sales are taken in secret by the Bundessicherheitsrat, or Federal Security Council, which consists of the chancellor, her chief of staff and seven other ministers. The German economics ministry publishes an annual arms report.
33. "German Weapons for the World: How the Merkel Doctrine Is Changing Berlin Policy", *Der Spiegel*, 3 December 2012, available at http://www.spiegel.de/interna-

tional/germany/german-weapons-exports-on-the-rise-as-merkel-doctrine-takes-hold-a-870596.html

34. Stockholm International Peace Research Institute, data on suppliers and recipients of major conventional weapons, 2006–10, available at http://www.sipri.org/yearbook/2011/06/06A
35. Bundesministerium für Wirtschaft und Technologie, Bericht der Bundesregierung über ihre Exportpolitik für konventionelle Rüstungsgüter im Jahre 2011. Rüstungsexportbericht 2011, September 2012, available at http://www.sipri.org/research/armaments/transfers/transparency/national_reports/germany/germany-2011
36. Robert Cooper, "The post-modern state and the world order", Demos, 2000, available at http://www.demos.co.uk/files/postmodernstate.pdf
37. Cooper, "The post-modern state and the world order", p. 37.
38. Ibid.
39. On hard and soft power, see Joseph S. Nye, *Soft Power: The Means To Success In World Politics* (New York: PublicAffairs, 2004).
40. The remainder of this section draws extensively on arguments I have made elsewhere. See Hans Kundnani, "Germany as a geo-economic power", *Washington Quarterly*, 34:3 Summer 2011, pp. 31–45, available at http://csis.org/files/publication/twq11summerkundnani.pdf
41. Edward Luttwak, "From geopolitics to geo-economics", *The National Interest*, Summer 1990, pp. 17–24. Reprinted in *The New Shape of World Politics* (New York: Norton, 1999), pp. 177–186, here p. 177.
42. Luttwak, "From geopolitics to geo-economics", p. 178.
43. Ibid. p. 180.
44. Ibid. p. 185.
45. Ibid.
46. See Mark Leonard, *What Does China Think?* (London: Fourth Estate, 2008), pp. 84–6.

CONCLUSION: GEO-ECONOMIC SEMI-HEGEMONY

1. Jürgen Habermas, "Germany's mindset has become solipsistic", *Guardian*, 11 June 2010, available at http://www.guardian.co.uk/commentisfree/2010/jun/11/germany-normality-self-absorption
2. This section draws extensively on arguments I have made elsewhere. See Hans Kundnani, "Was für ein Hegemon?", *Internationale Politik*, May/June 2012, pp. 21–25, available at https://zeitschrift-ip.dgap.org/de/ip-die-zeitschrift/archiv/jahrgang-2012/mai-juni/was-für-ein-hegemon (also in English as "What hegemon?", IP Global, 54 May 2012, available at https://ip-journal.dgap.org/en/ip-journal/topics/what-hegemon)

3. See for example Stefan Kornelius, "Hegemon wider Willen", *Süddeutsche Zeitung*, 28 November 2010, available at http://www.sueddeutsche.de/politik/euro-krise-hegemon-wider-willen-1.1028932; Christoph Schönberger, "Hegemon wider Willen. Zur Stellung Deutschlands in der Europäischen Union", *Merkur*, January 2012; William E. Paterson, "The Reluctant Hegemon? Germany Moves Centre Stage in the European Union", *Journal of Common Market Studies*, 49: 1, September 2011, pp. 57–75.
4. Radek Sikorski, "Poland and the future of the European Union", Berlin, 28 November 2011, available at http://www.msz.gov.pl/files/docs/komunikaty/20111128BERLIN/radoslaw_sikorski_poland_and_the_future_of_the_eu.pdf
5. Rede des Bundesministers der Finanzen Dr. Wolfgang Schäuble an der Université Paris-Sorbonne, 2 November 2010, available at http://www.bundesfinanzministerium.de/nn_88146/DE/Presse/Reden-und-Interviews/20101102-Sorbonne.html
6. On the idea of a "cooperative hegemon", see Thomas Pedersen, *Germany, France and the Integration of Europe* (London and New York: Pinter, 1998).
7. Several German historians have written about the re-emergence of German "semi-hegemony" in Europe. See Andreas Wirsching, "Der große Preis", *Frankfurter Allgemeine Zeitung*, 11 September 2012, available at http://www.faz.net/aktuell/feuilleton/debatten/europas-zukunft/gastbeitrag-zur-zukunft-europas-der-grosse-preis-11886472.html; Andreas Rödder, "Dilemma und Strategie", *Frankfurter Allgemeine Zeitung*, 13 January 2013, available at http://www.faz.net/aktuell/politik/die-gegenwart/europa-dilemma-und-strategie-12023770.html; Dominik Geppert, "Halbe Hegemonie: Das deutsche Dilemma", *Aus Politik und Zeitgeschichte*, 6–7/2013, 4 February 2013, available at http://www.bpb.de/apuz/154378/halbe-hegemonie-das-deutsche-dilemma?p=all; Dominik Geppert, "Die Rückkehr der deutschen Frage", *Journal of Modern European History*, Volume 11, Number 3, August 2013, pp. 272–278.
8. Email correspondence with Lucio Caracciolo.
9. See for example A. Wess Mitchell and Jan Havranek, "Atlanticism in Retreat", *The American Interest*, November/December 2013, available http://www.the-american-interest.com/article-bd.cfm?piece=1502
10. George Soros, "The Tragedy of the European Union and How to Resolve It", *New York Review of Books*, 27 September 2012, available at http://www.nybooks.com/articles/archives/2012/sep/27/tragedy-european-union-and-how-resolve-it/?pagination=false
11. On the idea of a "nightmare of coalitions" within the eurozone, see also Proissl, "Why Germany fell out of love with Europe", p. 19; David Marsh, *Europe's Deadlock. How the Euro Crisis Could Be Solved—and Why It Won't Happen* (New Haven and London: Yale University Press, 2013), p. 116.

12. Kenneth Dyson, "Germany, the Euro Crisis and the Future of Europe: Europe's Reluctant and Vulnerable Hegemonic Power", manuscript shared by author, p. 14.
13. Winkler, *The Long Road West. Volume II*, p. 580.
14. Heinrich August Winkler, "Greatness and Limits of the West. The History of an Unfinished Project", Ralf Dahrendorf Lecture, London School of Economics, 7 October 2010, available at http://www.lse.ac.uk/europeanInstitute/LEQS/LEQSPaper30.pdf
15. "Old Alliances or New Partnerships?" *IP Global Edition*, September/October 2011, p. 4. The poll was carried out for *Internationale Politik* by Forsa in August 2011.
16. Infratest dimap, Eine Umfrage zur politischen Stimmung im Auftrag der ARD-Tagesthemen und der Tageszeitung Die Welt, April 2014, available at http://www.infratest-dimap.de/uploads/media/dt1404_bericht.pdf
17. Jacques Schuster, "Deutschland verabschiedet sich langsam vom Westen", 22 April 2014, available at http://www.welt.de/debatte/kommentare/article127197927/Deutschland-verabschiedet-sich-langsam-vom-Westen.html; Christiane Hoffmann and René Pfister, "Part of the West? 'German Leftists Have Still Not Understood Putin'", Spiegel Online, 27 June 2014, available at http://www.spiegel.de/international/germany/interview-with-historian-heinrich-winkler-about-germany-and-the-west-a-977649.html. See also John Vincour, "Germany Turns Against the West on Russia", *Wall Street Journal*, 28 April 2014, available at http://online.wsj.com/news/articles/SB10001424052702303939404579529341282445718

INDEX

INDEX